Dr. Nasser B. Abulhasan

Light, Sight and Architecture

An approach to designing for the optimum by capturing the minimum

LAP LAMBERT Academic Publishing

Impressum / Imprint
Bibliografische Information der Deutschen Nationalbibliothek: Die Deutsche Nationalbibliothek verzeichnet diese Publikation in der Deutschen Nationalbibliografie; detaillierte bibliografische Daten sind im Internet über http://dnb.d-nb.de abrufbar.

Bibliographic information published by the Deutsche Nationalbibliothek: The Deutsche Nationalbibliothek lists this publication in the Deutsche Nationalbibliografie; detailed bibliographic data are available in the Internet at http://dnb.d-nb.de.

Coverbild / Cover image: www.ingimage.com

Verlag / Publisher:
LAP LAMBERT Academic Publishing
ist ein Imprint der / is a trademark of
OmniScriptum GmbH & Co. KG
Bahnhofstraße 28, 66111 Saarbrücken, Deutschland / Germany
Email: info@lap-publishing.com

Herstellung: siehe letzte Seite /
Printed at: see last page
ISBN: 978-3-8383-9376-6

Zugl. / Approved by: Graduate School of Design, Harvard University, Cambridge, MA, USA and. Diss. 2007

Light, Sight and Architecture

An approach to designing for the optimum by capturing the minimum

Table of Contents

Summary

Light, Sight and Architecture
An approach to designing for the optimum by capturing the minimum

Light is essential for many forms of life. The psychological and physiological effects of daylight, namely, promoting health and happiness, work productivity, efficiency and many more has made daylight research one of the central cornerstones of architectural research.

Many contemporary researches have been at the forefront of technological innovation and trials in societies with particularly overcast skies. Much has been done in this field that has reshaped the field of design altogether. This research has focused on capturing the maximum daylight. In this context, this author has developed an alternative understanding of the goal and proposed means to providing optimum day lighting. The motivation to develop a more differentiated framework for improve day lighting in buildings has become the main driver of this research.

The author's work is particularly interested in designing in arid climates and abundant sunlight, especially the Arabian Gulf. Contemporary research's motivation to 'capturing the maximum' day lighting in buildings is misdirected in such a society. Yet, the Arabian Gulf is filled with mis-applied research, with examples that focus on exactly that – without an exploration of the root cause of such an approach, developed in a context of intense overcast skies such as Germany or the United Kingdom.

Another component of daylight design is that its relationship to the physiology of the human eye as it responds to light, and the overall human perception of spaces has not been explored enough in arid climates. The human eye and its reaction to its surrounding light spaces are important factors in this dialogue.

Therefore, challenges that we, designers and architects in arid climates, are compounded with are two fold:

Firstly is to approach the problem of daylight design in arid climates differently from the conventional methods of the West. The challenges faced in societies with abundant sunlight are intrinsically different than those faced in cold, overcast skies.

Secondly is to take into account, in this process, the role that the human eye plays in reacting to given spaces and its contribution, if at all, to overall daylight design.

In tackling these two distinct challenges, three types of experiments were conducted.

1. Built Test Facility: this experiential model includes evaluations on perceptions in controlled sequences of spaces designed through interviews, with subjects entering and working in differentiated space with controlled lighting.
2. Computational Model: this is analytical in nature, using a computer model to test different light measures.
3. Applied Research in Design (In site experiments): this includes actual built examples that test the journey that the hypothesis develops with each additional experiment.

After reviewing the current daylight design trends, and studying the physiology of the human eye as it responds to its surroundings, a clear misalignment is posed. The technology surrounding daylight design rarely takes into account visual perception. In fact, the research related to this field tries to tackle several problems, some more successfully than others such as energy conservation, or aesthetically enhancing a space by maximizing light penetration. In particular, since these technologies have been developed for climates that have minimal daylight, and by in large overcast skies, the issue of visual perception has not been emphasized.

This investigation asks questions not often asked by designers in arid climates. Are fully glazed windows the appropriate choice of design? How can we manage to reassess lighting design for the purpose of overall energy conservation? How can we, as architects, design responsibly and effectively, in environments that are evolving, and in particular, arid climates?

This research seeks to develop a more effective to daylight design in arid climates, informed by a more holistic and scientific understanding of human vision and perception.

Chapter I. Approaches to Lighting Design – Components and Impact

The Challenge of Designing in a World with Growing Energy Consumption

The field of design is compounded today with many challenges. In a planet that is witnessing one of its most tragic ecological imbalances, technology has spearheaded scientific and research efforts in the race to be more environmentally aware, responsible, and accountable.

The footprints of this race are everywhere to be seen. Whether it is in tightly monitored light sensors, or sophisticated building materials, designers, engineers, scientists, and academics have gotten very creative in trying to build spaces that are 'more green'. Designing in an environment with quickly depleting natural resources, the battle for energy conservation has covered significant ground. As global energy consumption is expected to increase by 54% in the next twenty years, more focus and attention is geared at curbing the large costs incurred in buildings.

In the United States, for instance, the Department of Energy estimates that 40% of energy used in the US is in the building sector. This includes electricity generation, of which 70% is consumed by buildings[1].

A main cost factor in energy consumption of buildings is lighting, amounting to almost 30% of overall cost. Space cooling, an important factor for arid climates, is approximately 12%[2]. These challenges are significant leading to the serious focus

[1] Department of Energy Website. www.eia.doe.gov
[2] Department of Energy Website. www.eia.doe.gov

academics, designers and engineers have placed on understanding and exploring the field of lighting.

Daylight Design:

In recent years, the wave of designing for maximum daylight penetration has swept the architecture field. One of the reasons for this movement is the strong correlation that has been found between increased daylight and human performance and efficiency. Increased daylight penetration is also believed to reduce the use of artificial light, hence decreasing costs. Even on the aesthetic level, a space penetrated by daylight is both admired and replicated. Enhancing user comfort, reducing power consumption for lighting and cooling and promoting overall quality are some of the main objectives of daylight design.

This has been one of the fastest growing angles within the field of architecture. The focus has shifted from facades that better insulate, to building material technologies that allow for more light and less heat, with specific measurements and sizes. In any account, design, dimensions, texture, angles and countless other factors have been scrutinized, and studied. All has been done in the quest to promote and improve on energy efficiencies.

"In a world newly concerned about carbon emissions, global warming, and sustainable design, the planned use of natural light in non-residential buildings has become an important strategy to improve efficiency by minimizing lighting, heating and cooling loads. The introduction of innovative, advanced day lighting systems can considerably reduce a building's electricity consumption and also significantly improve the quality of light in an indoor environment."[3]

Principles

Some of the elements of daylight design are window orientation, size, daylight controls and shading devices. These elements are manipulated and controlled to assess the optimum levels of illuminance, uniformity of light distribution and related light technical comfort values as defined by the minimum values in standards and directives [DIN].[4] These measurements are supplemented by the lighting designer's own personality and perception of the amount of light necessary given an interior space. In addition, the color of light and how it changes during the day and during the different seasons is also an influential factor. Careful attention is paid to glazing, not only to improve energy balance, but also to ensure that the color rendition is not affected.

Requirements for illumination[5]

Luminance: The photometric measure of the density of luminous intensity in a given direction. (candela per unit area [cd/m2]

Illuminance: The measure of the total luminous flux on a certain area – independent of what the eye perceives. (lux)

Daylight factor: the ratio of illuminance at a certain point (Ep) to the illuminance outdoors (Ea). D=Ep/Ea. This is of critical importance in the experiments that will be highlighted in later chapters.

---

[3] International Energy Agency, Daylighting in Buildings

[4] Lighting Designs. Principles, Implementation, and Case Studies. DETAIL Practice. Institut fur Internationale. Mucich: 2006

[5] Lighting Designs. Principles, Implementation, and Case Studies. DETAIL Practice. Institut fur Internationale. Mucich: 2006

These factors are the essential methods of analysis, thus determining the necessary values for daylight delivery. For instance, the recommended amount of illuminance in an office space is 300 – 500 lux. Hence a daylight factor of 3 to 5% is necessary "so that daylight and artificial lighting are balanced under overcast sky conditions."[6] Since these measures are part of Lighting Design Standards, they are perpetuated by lighting suppliers, lighting designers, engineers and architects. Countries of the Arabian Peninsula without fail follow these measures. They have infiltrated building codes and municipal measures of standards. Further description of the implementation and ramification of such measures in countries of the Arabian Peninsula, and more specifically, Kuwait and the United Arab Emirates will be covered in other chapters.
Some of the methods of calculation and simulation include RADIANCE, LIGHTSCAPE, DOE-2, ENERGY 10 and ADELINE[7]. These represent a small fraction of the many programs that exist to simulate quantitative daylight levels and qualitative renderings of architectural space.

With these parameters, some of the questions most commonly asked are:

How do we improve the experience of the end user? How does that affect productivity? How can we manage to reassess lighting design for the purpose of overall energy conservation? How can we, as architects, design responsibly and effectively, in environments that are evolving, and in particular, arid climates? How can we also ensure that factors such as conservation, labor productivity, and overall human experience are introduced in the process of design?

---

[6] Lighting Designs. Principles, Implementation, and Case Studies
[7] Benya. Heschong. "Advanced Lighting Guidelines". New Building Institute Inc. 2003

The Center for Building Performance and Diagnostics at Carnegie Mellon works on linking high performance buildings to increase worker heath and productivity, organizational flexibility, technological adaptability and energy and environmental effectiveness. One of the areas of careful study on the overall 'health' of the building is lighting control. In addition, the group also focuses on studying the inter-disciplinary interactions between air, temperature control, network access, interaction space, ergonomics and access to natural environment and identifying these weakness as stand alone, and as they relate to one another. In an interview by Better Bricks, Vivian Loftness, Head of the School of Architecture at Carnegie Mellon University in Pittsburg, refers to the role of the Advanced Building Systems Integration Consortium, a team focused on the development of higher performing buildings. This team explores the quality of the indoor environment and asks profound questions, most relevant for this work is: "Why does a building designed to allow for daylight have all the electrical lights on?"[8]

Loftness describes the challenges of calculating worker productivity in a commercial office environment, referring to absenteeism (unused sick days) as easier to calculate. (Productivity is classically measured through speed and accuracy in executing a specific task – yet creative work cannot be so easily measured). The national average in the United States is 3-5% (7-12 working days), low compared to other countries in the world. The ABSIC explores whether or not buildings, healthy or sick, have a role in overall absenteeism and what these implications are on the overall cost for the employer and employee turnover. This is such compelling work, and is such a widespread problem, that sick buildings have been estimated by the Environmental Protection Agency to cost

[8] Loftness, Vivian. Interview with Better Bricks. www.betterbricks.com

the US economy almost $60 billion annually[9]. These studies, at the forefront of research, weave the fabric of connecting the importance of daylight design to overall performance and productivity. The questions shift from being, "What's the cheapest light fixture?" to "What light fixture will provide the best benefit in a three-year, five-year, or 15-year life cycle?"[10]

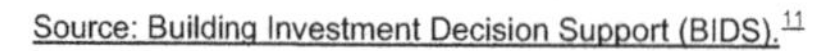
Source: Building Investment Decision Support (BIDS).[11]

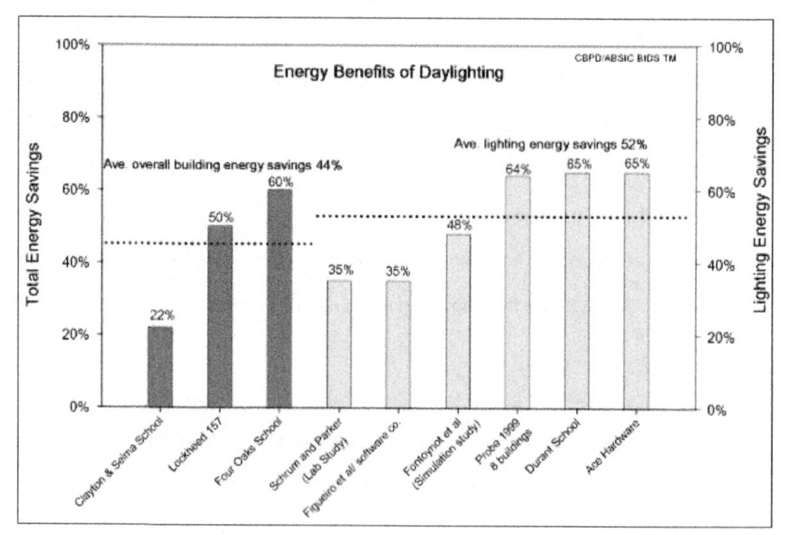

When testing energy benefits of daylighting, this diagram shows a saving of an average 44% and 52% for overall building energy savings and lighting energy saving respectively.

---

[9] Loftness, Vivian. Interview with Better Bricks. www.betterbricks.com
[10] Loftness, Vivian. Interview with Better Bricks. www.betterbricks.com
[11] Loftness. Hartkopf. Gurteken. "Building Investment Decision Support (BIDS) Cost Benefit Tool to Promote High Performance Components, Flexible Infrastructures and Systems Integration for Sustainable Commercial Buildings and Productive Organizations" Carnegie Mello University. Center for Building Performance and Diagnostics.

Daylight Design plays a critical role in saving overall costs.

Although it represents one of the many factors that can influence productivity, the below diagram from ABSIC / BIDS does demonstrate how significantly productivity can affect overall cost structure. Average savings of 5.5%, almost $2,475 per employee is significant. Adrian Leaman in England estimates "the potential impact for buildings on overall productivity as +12.5% (improved performance) and -17% (hampered performance) for an overall 30% change in worker performance in the healthy versus sick buildings."[12]

Source: Building Investment Decision Support (BIDS)[13]

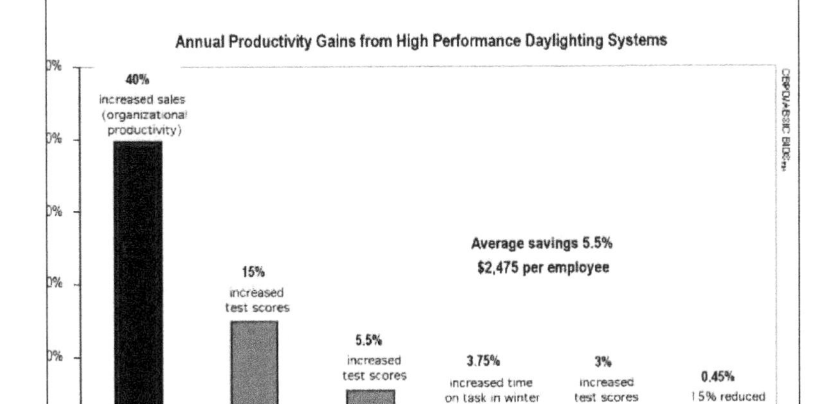

[12] Loftness. Hua. "Building Investment Decision Support (BIDS) Cost Benefit Tool to Promote High Performance Components, Flexible Infrastructures and Systems Integration for Sustainable Commercial Buildings and Productive Organizations. Page 16

[13] Loftness. Hartkopf. Gurteken. "Building Investment Decision Support (BIDS) Cost Benefit Tool to Promote High Performance Components, Flexible Infrastructures and Systems Integration for Sustainable Commercial Buildings and Productive Organizations" Carnegie Mello University. Center for Building Performance and Diagnostics. Page 23

This field has been at the forefront of much research as countless studies have been conducted on increasing overall efficiency and maximizing on productivity. This paper aims at studying the impact of these daylight design strategies on arid climates. I will explore the physiology of the process of sight, the complexities of perception as we try to design, and understanding the overall nuances of human perception in a given space. Special attention will be dedicated to understanding the challenges in lighting design in arid climates.

Bearing this framework in mind, and this particular angle in tackling the question of lighting, an experimental approach that studies the field of lighting through three main types of experiments was designed: a built test facility, computer simulated models, as well as in-site experiments. With the test facility, the main area of investigation is centered on qualitatively understanding, through interviews with subjects, the relationship between their perceptual experiences as it relates to the amount of light in the controlled space. As for the simulated computer models, the investigation is designed to quantitatively understand how the measurements of illuminance are influenced by the size of apertures and the North / South / East / West orientation. Lastly, the third experiment includes built case studies that test some of the learning of the earlier experiments.

The following chapters will first address the results of the conventional approaches to design, and in particular arid climates, the exploration of human vision and overall perception, and finally the experiments we have set forth.

Conventional Challenges to Lighting Design

Despite the tremendous upsides to introducing daylight design, there are also significant challenges that are further compounded if designed in arid climates. Particularly as the work space has grown more and more untraditional, that is, the typical paper-based work station has shifted. Today, the work space needs to be is compatible with all the activities that an employee would be engaged in. For instance, Video Display Terminals (VDT), in combination with paper-based tasks and project / team oriented working groups create a less predictable work environment and thus lighting necessities. Work stations are no longer static and multi-tasking even between VDTs and paper tasks require certain repositioning of not only artificial light, but careful attention to the way the windows are designed to integrate daylight.

The conventional approaches to lighting design have not always yielded their intended results.

"Daylight strategies and systems have not always lived up to their promise as energy efficiency strategies that enhance occupant comfort and performance." [14]

Daylight can produce uncomfortable solar glare and very high luminance reflections on display screens, both of which interface with good vision; thus affecting productivity

- Increase daylight means increase heat gain; more costs involving cooling mechanisms. Therefore, higher operating costs.
- This will cause excessive energy, which affects the already depleting environmental resource.

---

[14] International Energy Agency, Daylighting in Buildings

Therefore, the current approach of reducing construction and operating costs, preserving the depleting environmental resources, improving efficiency and comfort is not directly or accurately addressed by increasing daylight penetration into spaces.

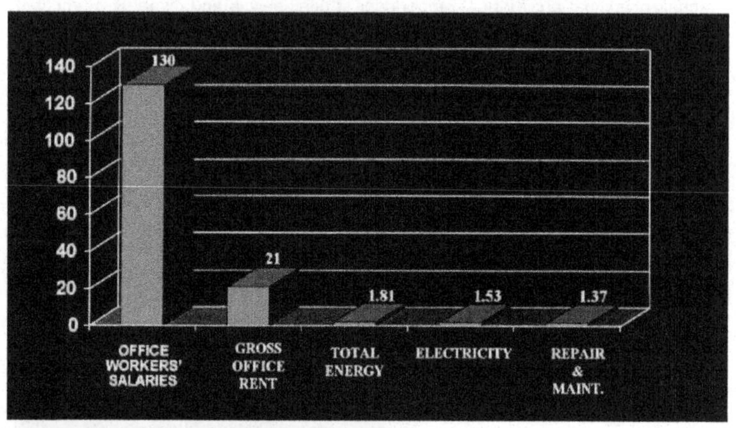

In addition to the challenges of meeting energy conservation objectives, daylight design can sometimes also contribute to heath effects.

Physiologically and perceptually, some of the most common problems related to inadequate or ineffective lighting are eyestrain or visual fatigue, ergonomic problems (screen reflections), headaches, and glare sensitivities[15]. Migraines have also been associated to inadequate or excessive lighting environments, fully impacting the overall health of the end user. Excessive luminance ratios and in particular, glare are prevalent issues in countries with arid climates, particularly if the work space employs fully glazed windows. The below images demonstrate the frequency of this use.

[15] Miller. "Vision and the Computerized Office". Herman Miller Inc. 2001

The current architectural practices in the Arabian Gulf are adopting mostly European and American designs. These images demonstrate the majority of new buildings being constructed in the Gulf. The buildings use excessive highly reflective tinted glass as a solution to reduce the heat gain and attempt to maintain external views for the end user. Unfortunately, the building codes currently specify the thermal conditions required by the façade in order to conserve energy consumed for HVAC. This architectural approach does not respond to the climatic issues, but poses solutions for a different problem altogether.

This work focuses on arid climates where the energy costs of conventional design have skyrocketed. However, not only is the existing approach to designing with light ill-conceived in arid climates, a direct 'copy-paste' approach has less than optimal results. Designing in arid climates requires a different method of designing with light. The current practices adopt the European and the American approach of fully glazed buildings with minimum understanding of abundance of sun light, and its effects. By importing these western approaches to design, spaces are lit excessively to compensate for the abundant daylight penetration. Both Kuwait and the United Arab Emirates present a particularly compelling argument with this regard.

Daylight design has encountered challenges in the West, and those are still under intense review and scrutiny. The relationship between cost effectiveness, productivity and energy conservation remains an ongoing debate. These methodologies, however, of daylight design that are prevalent in the West have far more serious implications in arid climates than they do in the West because of the climatic reality that arid climates face of abundant sunlight and intense heat. Implications of employing these principles in such climates are still difficult to quantify. It would be safe however, to conclude that these approaches severely harm measures of energy conservation. The following section will attempt to demonstrate this.

Chapter II. Consequences of Imported Lighting Design in Arid Climates

Kuwait:

Temperature: summer: 130-140 degrees Fahrenheit

Climate: dry desert; intensely hot summers; short, cool winter.

Designing in arid climates requires a different method of designing with light. The current practices adopt the European and the American approach of fully glazed buildings with minimum understanding of abundance of sun light, and its effects. By simply importing these western approaches to design, spaces are lit excessively to compensate for the abundant daylight penetration.

The operating cost of mechanically cooling these spaces, lighting it up with excessive artificial light, and attempting to minimize heat gain is so excessive, it represents the heaviest burden on owners and users.

Particularly in climates that are both very hot and very sunny, a different framework to designing with light is critical. Designers need to reinvent methodologies that are case and climate specific.

Unfortunately, societies of arid climates, and in particular, the Arabian Peninsula are climatically unconscious. They dedicate very little expertise and funding into research within this field. They rely heavily if not entirely on research conducted in the West. What further exacerbates the situation is that the consequence of the current approach to design with light is actually quite harmful. In addition, a significant distinction exists between daylight and sunlight.

Sunlight is much more prominent than daylight in arid climates, yet much more research and study (particularly in the West) has been dedicated to understanding the properties and prominence of *daylight,* in particular countries with overcast skies.

The severe climatic condition defines the weather in the Arabian Gulf, and in essence has paramount implications on the way buildings are designed, materials are chosen, and energy is consumed. In fact, an exorbitant amount of funds is spent on the production of electricity. Most of this energy is consumed by HVAC and lighting. Air conditioning installations absorb 60 to 70 percent of the consumed energy. As a consequence, many commercial companies have offered a variety of air conditioning units—capacities one to three tons—at very close range of prices without giving any attention to improve operative efficiency to lower power consumption. As a result, the battle to reduce the heat took a more commercial turn, where larger units meant better escape from the high temperature.

The recommendations in the "Energy Conservation Program" published by the Ministry of Electricity and Water in Kuwait specifically emphasize that: "Some new lighting systems and appliances are more energy-efficient than existing ones. Their use will reduce both peak loads and energy consumption."[16]

This shows a lack of understanding of approach to reducing the costs associated to lighting. By using simply an engineering perspective of reducing the energy consumption within buildings, the "Energy Conservation Program" does not suggest a different alternative to lighting design. The UAE on the other hand, is attempting to view the

[16] Ministry of Electricity and Water in Kuwait. www.moo.gov.kw

conservation battle a little less technically, and more intrinsically. This will be further elaborated on the section dedicated to the UAE.

The following examples represent typical internal spaces in office buildings in Kuwait and the UAE.

Emirates Tower Hotel, Dubai / United Arab Emirates

Photograph taken by N. Abulhasan

This hotel is one of the most successful and expensive business hotels in Dubai. The hotel rooms (approximately 35m.sq) have fully-glazed 6w X 3h meter windows, facing the east. As a result, the level of darkness in the room is significant.

Emirates Office Tower, Dubai / United Arab Emirates

Photographs taken by N. Abulhasan

This image shows the expansive use of artificial light, despite the large floor to ceilings windows. The level of luminance needs to be compensated through artificial light. The below images also demonstrate this fact.

Note: Intense Glare.

SOM Hilton, Mangaf / Kuwait

The sea facing rooms, with fully-glazed windows, are so bright that the use of the sheer curtains is needed to minimize the brightness, but simultaneously, the room is still perceived as dark. The excessive use of artificial light is needed to balance the brightness from the windows.

Photographs taken by N. Abulhasan

The below exhibits are in Kuwait and represent an office space – both with and without artificial light.

GIC Office Building / Kuwait City

Photograph taken by N. Abulhasan

These examples in the United Arab Emirates and Kuwait are demonstrative of a much larger looming architectural design challenge in the Arabian Gulf. The economic growth in these countries is staggering – the real estate sector [17]even peaks 8% of growth in the UAE, and in particular Dubai.

[17] www.uaeinteract.com

Yet, this approach leads to more construction costs, increased energy consumption, significant discomfort in the work space to name only a few disadvantages. A different approach is necessary amongst designers for arid climates as opposed to merely copying western designs which have a deficiency in daylight. Countries of the Arabian Peninsula do not have this problem – in fact, they have too much light infiltration.

Current research that discusses windows in high performance buildings continue to propagate techniques that are more applicable in colder, more overcast climates than in arid climates. This research, however, offers measures to mitigate some of the problems faced with this type of design in arid climates. These measures include more sophisticated daylight controls, shading devices, and window sizes, to name a few. Another method in dealing with this imported measure is "double skin façade". Is this technique even applicable in arid climates? Does is it address the problem at hand, namely, heat and solar gain due to fully glazed buildings?

Therefore, the challenges that are faced in Western climates are further exacerbated in arid climates.

A Case Study: The United Arab Emirates

General:

- Energy consumption per capita is the highest in the world
- Carbon emissions per capita is at least twice developed countries.
- Carbon emissions per capita is at least ten times higher than the world's annual average emission
- Construction and real estate is one of the fastest growing sectors in the world.
- Levels of CO2 emissions and energy use per square meter have been alarming- as a result of the contemporary buildings compared to the traditional buildings in the UAE.

Climatic Conditions in the UAE[18]

SUN CHART – ABU DHABI

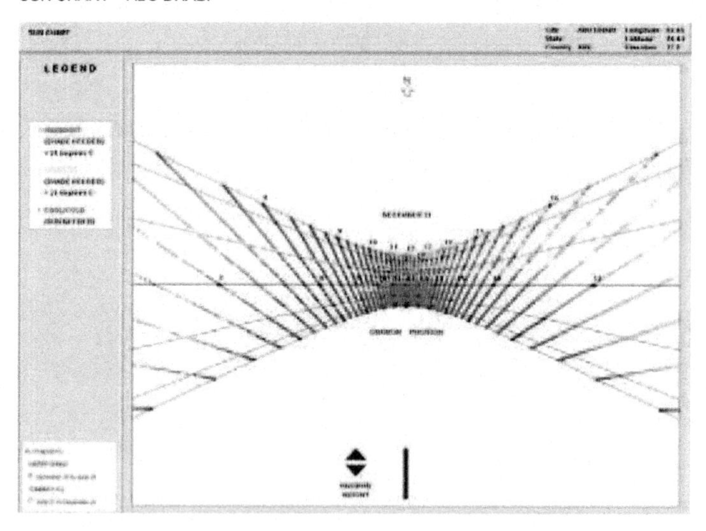

Sun chart shows the strong solar presence throughout the year. (Abundant sunlight).

---

[18] All Charts referring to climatic conditions in the UAE are produced by N. Abulhasan through Climate Consultant Software

SUN SHADING CHART – ABU DHABI

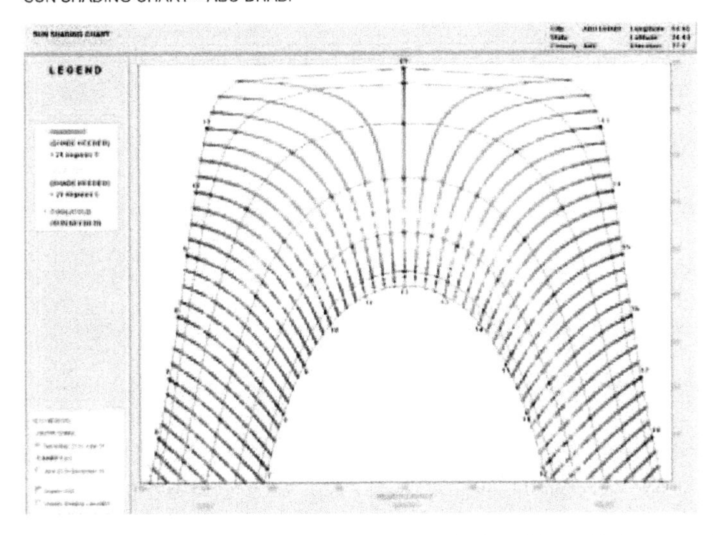

Sun Shade Chart shows the sun's movement throughout the day (lack of shadow / lack of overcast skies).

RADIATION RANGE – ABU DHABI

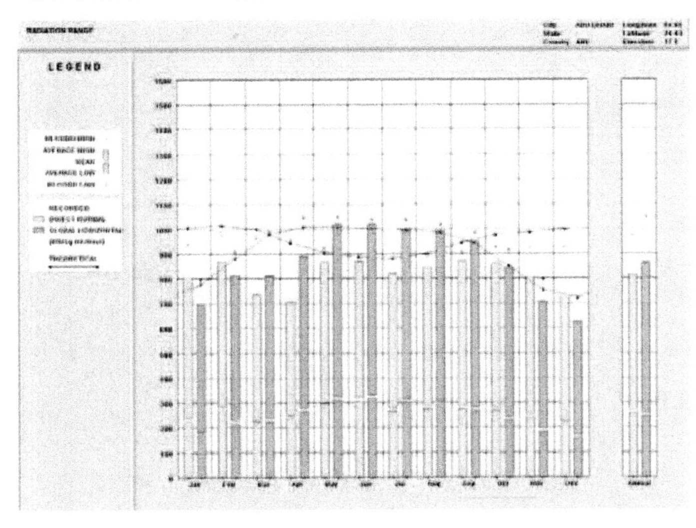

The Radiation Range table demonstrates intensity of solar rays – (implications on solar glare)

TEMPERATURE RANGE – ABU DHABI

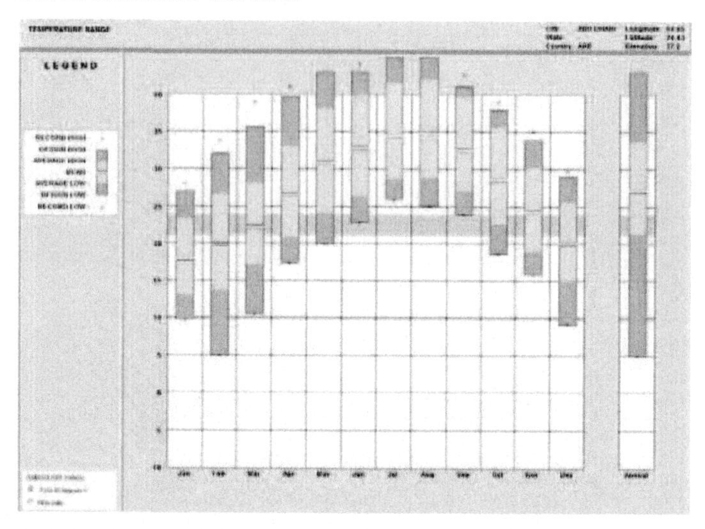

The Temperature Range table demonstrates the high temperatures throughout the year (solar heat gain, increased operating costs if western daylight design applied in arid climates.)

3D CHARTS – ABU DHABI

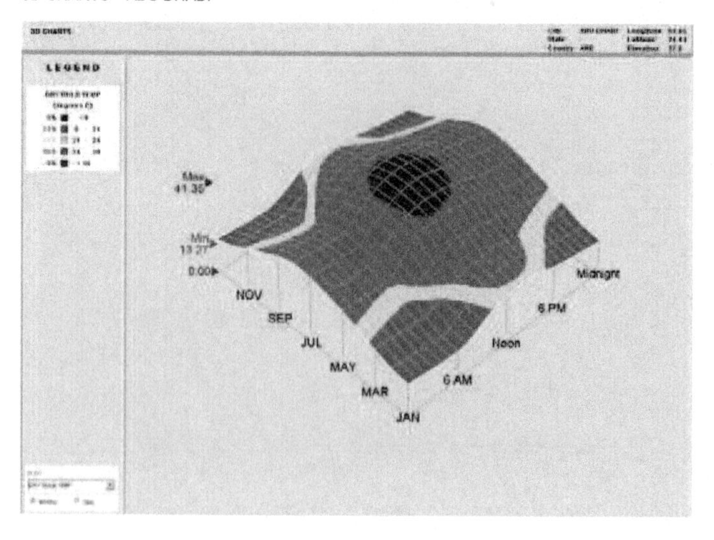

Climatic Changes through the time / year - the hottest and coolest times. Also emphasizes that most of the year is very warm.

PSYCHOMETRIC CHART – ABU DHABI

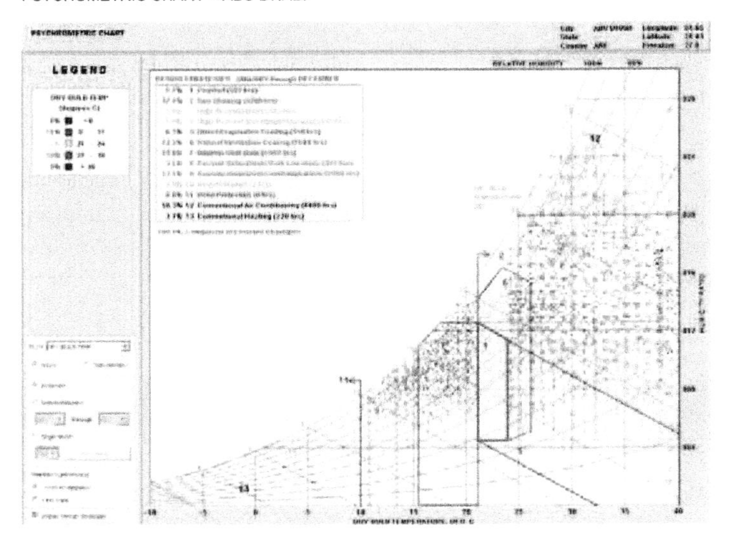

Photometric Chart highlights the comfort level which is extremely small – this window of opportunity necessary to be capitalized on.

WEATHER DATA SUMMARY – ABU DHABI

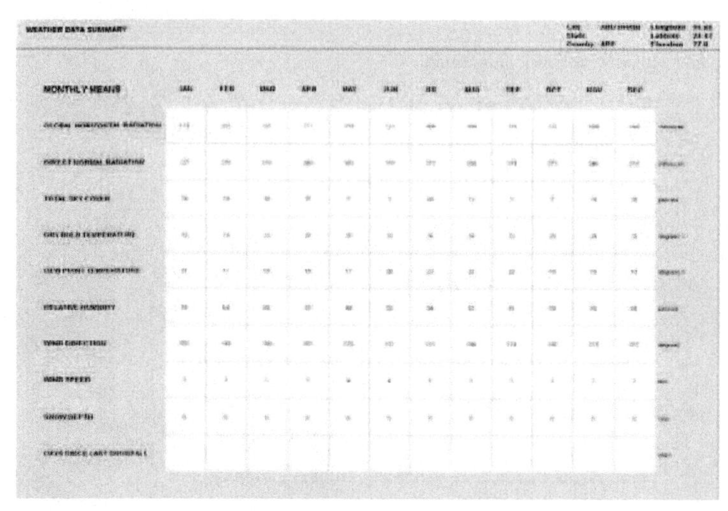

Weather Chart summarizes weather analysis in the UAE.

Energy and Electricity Consumption in the UAE

UAE's Energy and Electricity Consumption from 1980 to 2003[19]

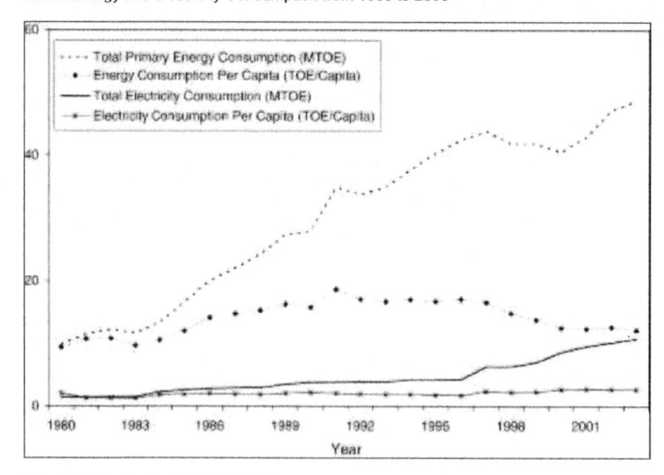

---

[19] Kazim. "Assessments of primary energy consumption and its environmental consequences in the United Arab Emirates." Renewable and Sustainable Energy Reviews. 2006 Elsevier Ltd.

In comparison to the rest of the world, the UAE's experience with both electricity consumption per capita, and total energy consumption is remarkable to note.

UAE's energy consumption per capita compared to other regions from 1980 to 2003[20]

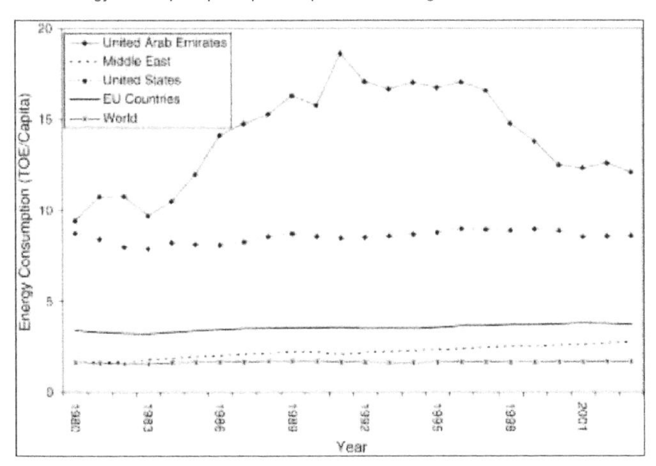

Electricity Consumption / Capita[21]

Electricity Consumption per Capita - (Kwhour/person)			
Region	**1990**	**2003**	**Growth**
Middle East & North Africa	1,126	1,920	4%
Europe	na	5,764	na
North America	12,124	13,629	1%
Developed Countries	na	7,701	na
World	2,067	2,436	1%
UAE	**8,766**	**11,435**	**2%**

[20] Kazim. "Assessments of primary energy consumption and its environmental consequences in the United Arab Emirates." Renewable and Sustainable Energy Reviews. 2006 Elsevier Ltd.
[21] Data retrieved from www.earthtrends.wri.org. CAGR calculations by N. Abulhasan

Total Energy Consumption 1990 – 2003[22]

Energy Consumption - (Kg of oil equivalent/person)				
Region	**1990**	**2000**	**2003**	**Growth**
Middle East & North Africa	368,746	584,104	657,367	5%
Europe	na	2,608,458	2,732,417	na
North America	2,137,002	2,554,348	2,543,482	1%
Central America & Carribean	172,400	209,729	222,307	2%
Developed Countries	na	6,102,435	6,233,332	na
Asia (exclude Middle East)	2,166,387	3,084,270	3,473,198	4%
World	8,623,148	9,942,517	10,571,717	2%
UAE	**22,545**	**35,791**	**42,482**	**5%**

For both Energy Consumption and Electricity consumption per capita, the UAE ranks very high. There are many reasons that can be attributed to this. One of which is the current approach to overall lighting design.

In a study comparing total energy use, artificial lighting and cooling energy used per square meter, results indicated that contemporary buildings in the UAE use almost six times more energy than traditional buildings. The main cause of this enormous consumption is attributed to the lack of energy saving featured in contemporary building features in the UAE[23].

Authorities in the UAE have recognized this and are slowly beginning to introduce standards that can mitigate this challenge. Dubai municipality for instance recently began imposing requirements to conserve electrical energy by mandating all major building contractors to use insulated bricks in all construction projects. It is estimated that conservation could amount to almost 40%[24]. This was previously an optional measure.

[22] Data retrieved from www.earthtrends.wri.org. CAGR calculations by N. Abulhasan
[23] Kazim. "Assessments of primary energy consumption and its environmental consequences in the United Arab Emirates." Renewable and Sustainable Energy Reviews. 2006 Elsevier Ltd.
[24] Kazim. "Assessments of primary energy consumption and its environmental consequences in the United Arab Emirates." Renewable and Sustainable Energy Reviews. 2006 Elsevier Ltd.

In 2004, the Ministry of Economy and Planning announced that power consumption in Dubai alone totaled 16,363 Gigawatts/hour, of which 70% was utilized in commercial and residential buildings.[25] The Ministry has begun to promote energy efficient buildings by acknowledging the importance of Indoor Environmental Quality (IEQ) and Indoor Air Quality (IAQ). Considering the intensive volume of cooling load, the Gulf and particularly the UAE is subjected to due to HVAC to keep buildings cool, IAQ has become a vital issue to ensure that healthy environments are kept at the highest levels. On October 1st 2007, the Emirates Green Building Council launched a proposed building sustainability assessment system for the UAE. The system is based on the US Green Building Council's (US GBC) Leadership in Energy and Environmental Design (LEED) rating system, with modifications made to account for the local environmental conditions. The proposed LEED Emirates system is currently lodged with the US GBC for evaluation. The main modifications in this proposed system include an increased emphasis on water conservation. In addition, certain adjustments were made to make the overall system more applicable for use in the UAE's construction sector.[26]

In an interview with Arabian Business Week, Jeff Willis, the EGBC Technical and Award Subcommittee coordinator said: "One of the reasons for using the LEED system as a basis was that we (the UAE) need the international market to know that this is serious." He considers this step as a starting point to slowly begin to introduce and customize UAE problems in a LEED system more applicable for the UAE. The objective is to apply this new system to 25 new buildings throughout the UAE after the ratification of LEED Emirates by September 2008.

---

[25] GulfNews. June 10, 2005

[26] Arabian Businessweek. October 1, 2007. Please note technical workshops are being held in Dubai and Abu Dhabi the month of October 2007 on this matter.

These represent steps taken in the right direction. Assessment of the impacts of these measures on overall cost and performance, productivity, and overall visual comfort will account for very compelling and pioneering future research.

Chapter III. Sight: Human Perception

Human Vision

This chapter will focus on the important physiological elements of human vision. The link however, between the way the human eye responds to light, and the conventional approaches to light design has not been explored in great depths. These two respective fields, that of neurology, and that of light design have remained unfamiliar to one another. Despite the critical role that the human eye plays in overall perception, in depth studies into the physiological developments and potential implications on perception in a three dimensional approach has merely skimmed the surface.

There are typically three ranges of illumination: scotopic, mesopic and photopic. Depending on the luminance level (log cd / m2) the different ranges are exercised. Typically, the scotopic range is focused on 'no color vision / poor acuity' whereas the photopic range includes 'good color vision and good acuity'. As for the mesopic level, there is still little known about this field but it is one of great interest since, " Relatively little is known about vision in the mesopic range, but this is increasingly a topic of interest because computer-based office environments with CRT displays and subdued lighting exercise the visual system's mesopic range."[27]

This chapter will attempt to explore this field, often reserved for medicine and in particular neurology through the prism of architectural design.

Vision is part of a complicated network of the total human sensory system, and is closely related to touch and hearing. Visual perception, which takes place as the observer

---

[27] Ferweda. Pattanaik. Shirley. "A Model of Visual Adaptation for Realistic Image Synthesis"

comes in contact and interacts with the visible surrounding, contributes to overall impression and experience of any given span. The focus of this chapter will remain on overall adaptation as opposed to the visual process as a whole – and in particular, the adaptation from light to dark and from dark to light. The physiological elements of responding to light rays in the process of adaptation include: the pupil, the rod and cone system, bleaching and regeneration of photo pigments, and neural processes.

Every day the human eye is compounded with thousands of different levels of luminosity. Its quick and seemingly seamless ability to shift between the different ranges of luminances still remains a mystery to us.

The pupil

The diameter of the pupil ranges between 7mm down to about 2 mm. This change is almost entirely dependent on the level of light. Quite simply, when there is a lot of light, the pupil shrinks, thus limiting the amount of light that enters the eye. When it is dark, the pupil enlarges trying to capture as much light as possible. This process is known as dark and light adaptation. It ranges between seconds for the transition to be complete, and can sometimes reach up to a few minutes for the entire process. This fascinating mechanism will be taken into account in our overall design methods, and will be further explored in the experiments.

The system of rods and cones

There are two kinds of light-receptor cells in the eye: the rods and cones. In the central region, the fovea, the receptors are packed exceedingly closer together, and all look like rods. There are typically 75 to 150 million rods in the retina, and 6 to 7 million cones. Each of these light receptors has a different function – the rods are extremely sensitive to light and provide the vision on the scotopic levels of illumination. The cones are less sensitive to light but provide color vision in the photopic levels of illumination.

The cones function in daylight conditions, and give color vision. The rods function under low illumination, giving vision only shades of grey. Daylight vision, using the cones of the retina, is referred to as *photopic* while the grey world given by the rods in dim light is called *scotopic*.

Bleaching and regeneration of photopigments

Pigment bleaching is a process where high light intensities depletes the photosensitive pigments in the rods and cones at a rate that is faster than the chemical processes that can restore them. Early studies have indicated that both dark and light adaptation was caused by pigment bleaching or pigment restoration. This theory, however, is not as strong because adaptation happens in both the rode and cone receptors where little bleaching occurs, and secondly, the phases in which this happens are so quick to catch up with the photochemical processes alone.

Neural Processes

This process is dependent on the chemical reactions produced by the action of light on the cell's photo-pigments. "This process acts very rapidly and accounts for changes in sensitivity over the first few seconds of adaptation."[28]

Seeing Brightness

Brightness is not just a simple matter of the intensity of light striking the retina. The brightness seen by a given intensity depends upon the state of adaptation of the eyes,

[28] Ferweda. Pattanaik. Shirley. "A Model of Visual Adaptation for Realistic Image Synthesis"

and also upon various complicated conditions determining the contrast of objects or of patches of light.

Brightness is a function not only of intensity of light falling on a given region of the retina at a certain time, but also of intensity of the light that the retina has been subjected to in the recent past. The eye is extremely sensitive to 'its history' and thus as the person moves through different levels of luminosity, it reacts in a very 'relative' format, based on the previous phase of luminosity it was in. This reaction will be manipulated in the designs that we have set because of the different phases of luminosity. Simply, the factors that affect the brightness include the intensity of the surrounding areas where given regions look brighter if its surroundings are dark, and a given colour looks more intense if it is surrounded by its complementary colour.

After all, brightness is a function of colour. If we shine lights of different colours, but the same intensity, into the eyes, the colours at the middle of the spectrum will look brighter than those of the ends.

Consider the following:

"Present the eye with a small fairly bright source: it will look at certain brightness, and the pupil will close to a certain size when the light is switched on. Now add a second, light. This is placed some way from the first, so that a different region of the retina is stimulated. What happens? Although the total intensity has increased, with the addition of the second light, the pupil does not close further as one might expect. Rather, it opens – to correspond to intensity between the first and the second light. It is evidentially set not by the total, but by the average illumination"[29]

As the eye becomes dark adapted, it trades its acuity in space and time for increase in sensitivity. With decreases of intensity, and the compensating dark adaptation, ability to make out fine detail is lost. This is partly due to the retina integrating over greater area and so a greater number of receptors.

The smallest difference in intensity which can be detected is directly proportional to the background intensity.

The following spectral luminosity curve[30] demonstrates this:

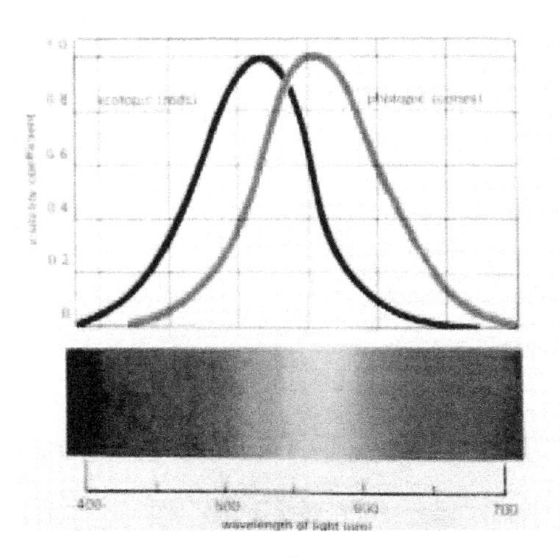

This shows how sensitivity of the eye to various wavelengths is different when the eye is light adapted. The black curve shows that the maximum sensitivity shifts along the spectrum when the eye is dark adapted. The red curve shows sensitivity when the eye is light adapted.

---

[29] Gregory. "Eye and Brain, The Psychology of Seeing"; page 89
[30] Gregory. "Eye and Brain. The Psychology of Seeing"

Adaptation

As a person moves through a building, the eyes experience a moment by moment transformation. This involuntary process of responding and adapting to varying brightness values of successive spaces is remarkable in its accuracy, fineness and speed.

In and out of dark quarters, as well as in and out of intense brightness of unfiltered daylight, these changes in brightness sometimes are severe and occur suddenly, and the eye is forced to adapt accordingly.

Light Adaptation: when the eye leaves the dark and enters bright surrounding, the pupil contracts, letting much less light into the retina. If the viewer had been in total darkness some time is required for adaptation to the light. Light adaptation happens within the scotopic range of the rod system and is extremely rapid. "More than 80% of sensitivity recovery occurs within the first 2 seconds, and nearly 75% happens within the first 200 ms."[31]

Dark Adaptation: when the eye leaves a well lit area to a dark surrounding, the iris expands allowing for as much light as possible to enter. Dark adaptation typically requires a few minutes. "Visually, dark adaptation is experienced as the temporary blindness that occurs when we go rapidly from photopic to scotopic levels of illumination. The relatively slow time-course of dark adaptation means that vision can be impaired for several minutes when we move quickly from high illumination to low ones."[32]

---

[31] Ferweda. Pattanaik. Shirley. "A Model of Visual Adaptation for Realistic Image Synthesis"
[32] Ferweda. Pattanaik. Shirley. "A Model of Visual Adaptation for Realistic Image Synthesis"

The below figure shows the time course of adaptation between rods and cones.

The red curve shows how the cones cells adapt, while the black curve shows the rod adaptation, which is slower and proceeds to greater sensitivity. In dim light only the rods are functional, while they are probably inhibited in brighter light by the active cones.

Trajectory of Light Sensitivity over time[33]

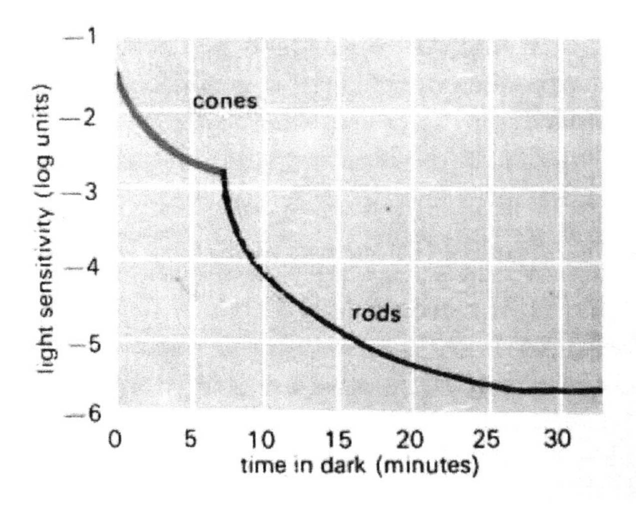

The below figure[34] demonstrates the concept of dark and light adaptation:

[33] Gregory. "Eye and Brain. The Psychology of Seeing"
[34] Gregory. "Eye and Brain. The Psychology of Seeing"

The part of the grey ring against the black appears somewhat lighter than the rest of the ring against the white background. This effect is enhanced when a thread is placed across the ring, along the black and white junction. "…Because of adaptation and expectation, we need more artificial light in many interior spaces during the day than at night, to balance the higher levels so that the interior does not appear dim and gloomy."[35]

Consider the following:

You are on the Las Vegas strip on a bright sunny summer day. You enter the lobby of Ceasars Palace. As you enter, you suddenly experience an overall dimness, despite the bright artificial and natural light that floods the lobby. Why is this the case? Why is the lobby so suddenly dark?

Quite simply, when you are strolling outside, your pupil is small – as you enter the lobby, it suddenly expands to try and absorb as much of the light rays as possible, which

[35] Lam, William. "Perception and Lighting As Forgivers For Architecture", New York, US: McGraw-Hill Book Company, 1977. (page 48)

perhaps don't amount to more than 1,000 lux. This large discrepancy in the lux factor (outside is probably 10,000 lux) is what creates the uncomfortable darkness that you experience when you enter the lobby.

Adaptation and Design

The implications of light or dark adaptation are not so much for lighting design of singular architectural spaces, but for illuminating the space that participates in a sequence of lighted spaces, because the ease or difficulty of light or dark adaptation will determine the visual comprehension, pleasantness, or discomfort experienced by moving from one space into another.

The architectural and lighting designers should avoid creating situations where the eye must adapt suddenly to excessive changes of light and dark.

Chapter IV. Hypothesis

After reviewing the current daylight design trends, and studying the physiology of the human eye as it responds to its surroundings, a clear misalignment is posed. The technology surrounding daylight design rarely takes into account visual perception. In fact, the research related to this field tries to tackle several problems, some more successfully than others such as energy conservation, or aesthetically enhancing a space by maximizing light penetration. In particular, since these technologies have been developed for climates that have minimal daylight, and by in large overcast skies, the issue of visual perception has not been emphasized. Outdoor illuminance in counties such as Germany and the United Kingdom (where the majority of daylight research is conducted) reaches approximately 5000 – 20000 lx in overcast skies. Due to the link drawn between increased productivity and overall ambience, research has focused on maximizing daylight into a given space. For instance, the intelligent facade with daylight controls is a technology that has to a very large degree focused on increasing daylight penetration.

In arid climates, however, there is no shortage of abundant sunlight. In fact, illuminance levels range from 20000 to 100000 lx. Yet, the technologies used for daylight design are primarily imported from climates that have the exact opposite problem. It is unfortunate that designs in arid climates, and in particular, countries of the Arabian Gulf simply do not address the problems at hand – that is the problems of designing in arid climates. Designs are limited to a myopic interpretation of how to address some of the problems that are faced: For example, fully glazed windows will be tinted to limit heat gain and sun glare. But the fully glazed approach remains, and countries of the Arabian Gulf continue to implement strategies that are designed for different circumstances and different problems altogether. This has been covered more extensively in earlier chapters. Needless to say, designing in arid climates has not taken into account human perception of surrounding space.

Due to these parameters, and our particular study of the human eye, several experiments were conducted to better understand whether or not a relationship exists between the human perception and daylight.

Some of the questions that we have posed:

Does the size of aperture affect how much we can see?

Does the frequency of luminaries contribute to an enhancement of perception?

What is the significance of a threshold?

How does it contribute to the overall experience?

What is the relationship between the sequence of movement from one space to another as it relates to the human eye?

These are some of the many questions that were posed as we tried to better understand the relationship between the human eye and daylight design.

The physiology of the human eye and its response to light, and in particular, light and dark adaptation that we explored in the earlier chapter, remains at a distance from extensive research on conventional daylight design.

In order to address the relationship between human perception and conventional daylight design, three types of analysis were conducted:

1. A controlled experiment
2. A computer simulation
3. In site experiments

To govern our experiments, the following variables were highlighted to understand this relationship. These variables are significant due to their importance in design.

They are the following:

- Room Size
- Room Shape
- Surface Reflectance
- Number of Sources of Luminance
- Location of Sources of Luminance
- Luminance of the entry field of view (X and Y Axis)
- Luminance of the entry field of view (Z Axis)
- Observer Location and Line of Sight
- Size of Aperture
- Frequency of Luminaires
- Contrast
- Color of Surfaces

These elements are trying to relate between human perception and daylight design. The next sections will detail our experiments with this regard.

SECTION A: CONTROLLED EXPERIMENT – TEST FACILY

Definition:

Building a full scale "Manager's Office" to quantify light measurements in relationship to the perceptual qualities within an office space.

Experiment Methodology

Constants:

1. Wall color / texture (White, non-reflective / Smooth)
2. 80cm x 200cm table surface
3. Human eye; sitting position
4. Structure Height from ground 30cm
5. Panels 50cm x 50cm
6. Ceiling height 3m
7. Room Dimension 4.5m x 3m

Variables:

1. Room Size
2. Room Shape
3. Surface Reflectance
4. Number of Sources of Luminance
5. Location of Sources of Luminance
6. Luminance of the entry field of view (X and Y Axis)
7. Luminance of the entry field of view (Z Axis)
8. Observer Location and Line of Sight

9. Size of Aperture
10. Frequency of Luminaires
11. Contrast
12. Color of Surfaces

Subjects in the Study[36]:

Ten subjects were interviewed.

Assumptions:

This prototype was governed by the following assumptions:

- Relationship between the size of the window and the amount of light entering a space – it was believed that the larger the opening, the more light will enter the space, hence, the brighter the space.
- The relationship between the amount of actual light and the perceived light
- The orientation of the window will change the perceived light

Experimental Method

Facility Details

A prototype standard private office space in downtown Kuwait which was completed in January 2005.

To evaluate day lighting, this full-scale, outdoor mockup was built in a parking lot in 'Bneid-al-Gar', State of Kuwait. The mock up reproduced a typical 3m X 4.5m manager's office. It was located at latitude 29.30N and longitude 48.00E and its orientation could be modified since it was built on a rotating base.

The view immediately out of the windows was of a parking lot with a grey concrete surface (ground surface reflectance 0.05 - .010).

The interior finish floor height was 30cm above the ground.

[36] Refer to Appendix A for contact details and actual interviews.

The interior day lit space (Figure B1) was 4.5m deep, 3m wide. The ceiling height at the window wall was 3m.

One type of office furniture was installed in the mockup. Desk surface was white composite material (r=0.84), the interior walls and ceiling are mdf wood panels painted matt white ral 9010 (r-0.87). The floor was composed of plywood panels on a 8cm X 8cm wooden caucus studs. Refer to B2, B3, B4, B5, B6 and B7.

The space was not conditioned.

Facade Description

The mdf wood panels' façade was designed on a 50cm X 50cm floor-to-ceiling grid structure. The panels could be removed to create a vision window. This is supported by a wooden caucus sub-frame of 4cm x 4cm. Refer to B8, B9, B10, B11, B12 and B13.

Panel Description

The panels are 50cm x 50cm held by horizontal mdf studs, which created the necessary support to maximize mobility flexibility in creating the desired openings. Refer to B14, B15, B16, B17

Shading and Lighting Systems Description

None

Monitoring Data

A portable light meter was used in the mockup to monitor interior lighting levels throughout the day.

Data was recorded every 20 minutes between 12pm and 3pm on December 21, 2005. March 21, 2006, June 21, 2006 and September 21, 2006.

All data was sampled and recorded in Standard Time within a few milliseconds of the time stamp.

Interior horizontal illuminations were monitored with photometric sensors on the desk surface, above finished floor.

Methods of data analysis

Interviewing subjects in the physical model [37]

The approach began in trying to asses perceived light within the space, depending on the opening. Subjects Bader, Muthla and Mohammed volunteered to help guide this study.

Images B18, B19, B20, B21, B22, B23, B24, and B25 demonstrate the manipulation of the panels to understand the relationship between the amount of light, and the perceived light. Refer to the questionnaire attached for clarity on how the perceived light was interpreted by the three subjects.

---

[37] Refer to Appendix A for contact details and actual interviews.

Experiment Results

Two main findings based on our subjects:

- The relationship between actual light in a given space and perceived light is not significant.
- The subjects perceived the brightness or dimness of the given space to a large extent on the brightness of the space they were in before. This concept of relativity has defined the findings, and translated into the design techniques used in the case studies.

Experiments	Room Size	Room Shape	Surface Reflectance	Number of Sources of Luminance	Location of Sources of Luminance	Luminance of the entry field of view **(X and Y Axis)**	Luminance of the entry field of view **(Z axis)**	Observer Location and Line of Sight	Size of Aperture	Frequency of Luminaires	Contrast	Color of Surfaces
	Variables											
Test Facility									IL		IL	

Color Key	
	Significant
	Less Significant
	Not Significant
IL	Influential Learning

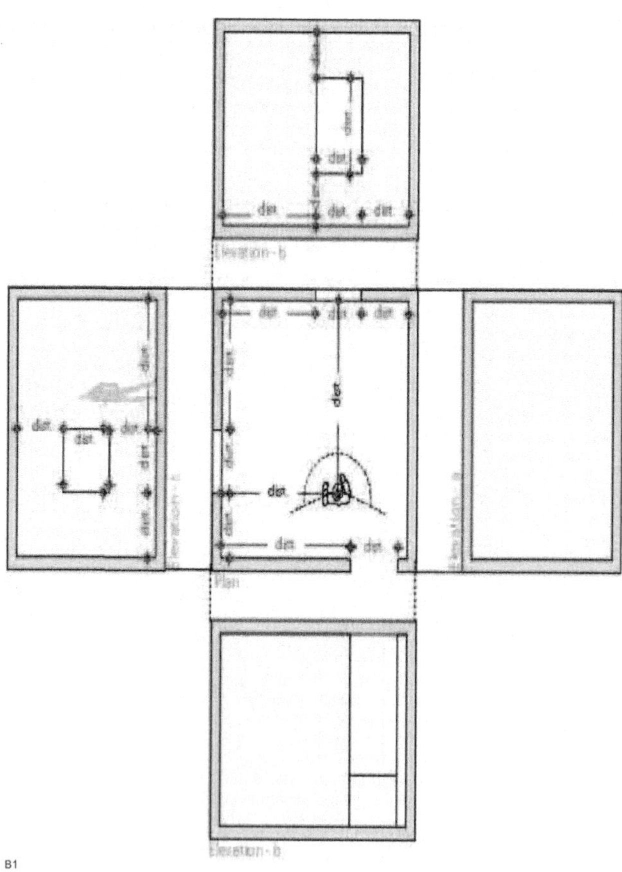

B1

B2
B7
B3
B8
B4
B9
B5
B10
B6
B11

B12
B18
B13
B19
B14
B21
B23
B15
B22
B16
B17
B24

Experiments	Variables											
	Room Size	Room Shape	Surface Reflectance	Number of Sources of Luminance	Location of Sources of Luminance	Luminance of the entry field of view **(X and Y Axis)**	Luminance of the entry field of view **(Z axis)**	Observer Location and Line of Sight	Size of Aperture	Frequency of Luminaires	Contrast	Color of Surfaces
Test Facility									IL		IL	

Color Key	
	Significant
	Less Significant
	Not Significant
IL	Influential Learning

B26

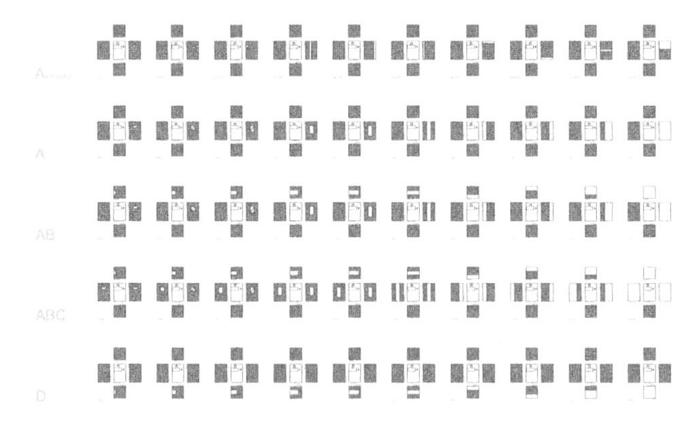

B25

SECTION B: COMPUTER SIMULATION (North / South / East / West)

Definition:

Designing a full scale "Manager's Office" to quantify light measurements through Lightscape.

Experiment Methodology

Constants:

1. Wall color / texture (White, non-reflective / Smooth)
2. 80cm x 200cm table surface
3. Structure Height from ground 30cm
4. Panels 50cm x 50cm
5. Ceiling height 3m
6. Room Dimension 4.5m x 3m

Variables:

- Room Size
- Room Shape
- Surface Reflectance
- Number of Sources of Luminance
- Location of Sources of Luminance
- Luminance of the entry field of view (X and Y Axis)
- Size of Aperture

Assumptions:

This prototype was governed by the following assumptions:

- Relationship between the size of the window and the amount of light entering a space – it was believed that the larger the opening, the more light will enter the space, hence, the brighter the space.
- The orientation of the window will change the amount of light.

Experimental Method

The computer model was designed to calculate the amount of luminosity inside the box depending on the size and location of the window.

Within this model, we were able to rotate the building and simultaneously test the window sizes on four different orientations.

To evaluate day lighting, a 3D model was built on Autocad and was transferred to Lightscape to study the lighting conditions. The model reproduced a typical 3m X 4.5m manager's office. It was located at latitude 29.30N and longitude 48.00E and its orientation could be easily modified. The model is a flexible model that allowed is to easily manipulate the number of panels and sizes to study the amount of light in the space. The model was rotated across four different orientations to analyze potential differences. The prototype represents a standard private office space in downtown Kuwait.

One type of office furniture in the prototype was used. Desk surface was white composite material (r=0.84), the interior walls and ceiling are painted matt white (r-0.87).

Facade Description

The façade was designed on a 50cm X 50cm floor-to-ceiling grid structure. The panels could be easily manipulated to create openings.

Panel Description

None

Shading and Lighting Systems Description

None

Monitoring and methods of data analysis

A photometric analysis was produced.

Experiment Results

The computer findings do not affect perception because it is digital space. Measuring light illuminations does not explain how light is perceived – the mere measurement in relation to the human eye is not understood.

Experiments	Variables											
	Room Size	Room Shape	Surface Reflectance	Number of Sources of Luminance	Location of Sources of Luminance	Luminance of the entry field of view **(X and Y Axis)**	Luminance of the entry field of view **(Z axis)**	Observer Location and Line of Sight	Size of Aperture	Frequency of Luminaires	Contrast	Color of Surfaces
Three D Model North				IL					IL			

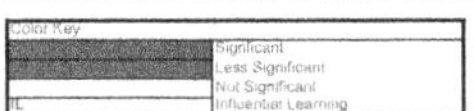

Color Key	
	Significant
	Less Significant
	Not Significant
IL	Influential Learning

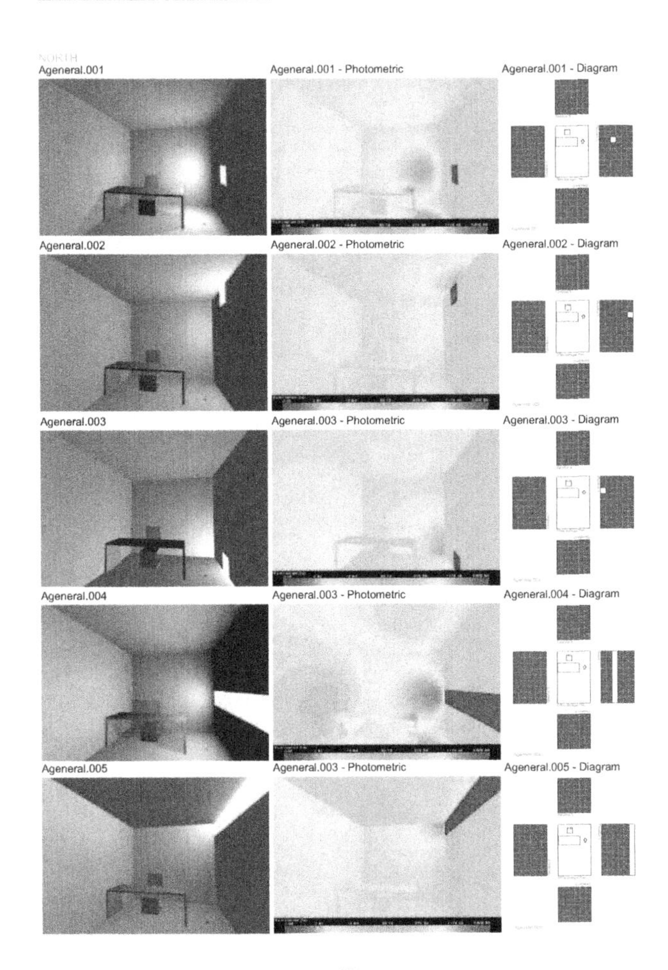

Experiments	Variables											
	Room Size	Room Shape	Surface Reflectance	Number of Sources of Luminance	Location of Sources of Luminance	Luminance of the entry field of view **(X and Y Axis)**	Luminance of the entry field of view **(Z axis)**	Observer Location and Line of Sight	Size of Aperture	Frequency of Luminaires	Contrast	Color of Surfaces
Three D Model North				IL					IL			

Color Key	
	Significant
	Less Significant
	Not Significant
IL	Influential Learning

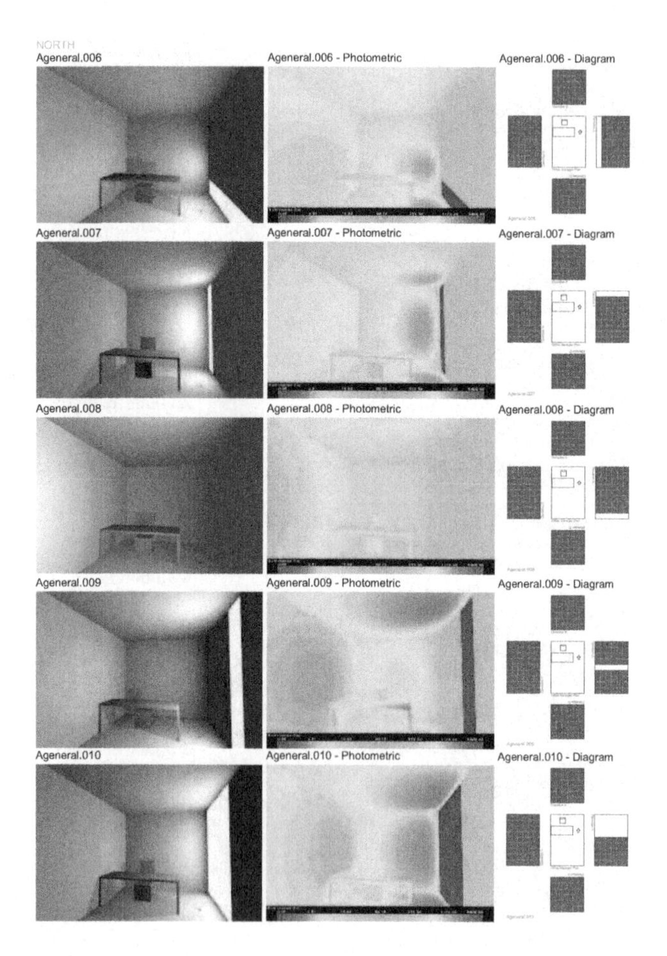

Experiments	Variables											
	Room Size	*Room Shape*	*Surface Reflectance*	*Number of Sources of Luminance*	*Location of Sources of Luminance*	*Luminance of the entry field of view* ***(X and Y Axis)***	*Luminance of the entry field of view* ***(Z axis)***	*Observer Location and Line of Sight*	*Size of Aperture*	*Frequency of Luminaires*	*Contrast*	*Color of Surfaces*
Three D Model South				IL					IL			

Color Key	
	Significant
	Less Significant
	Not Significant
IL	Influential Learning

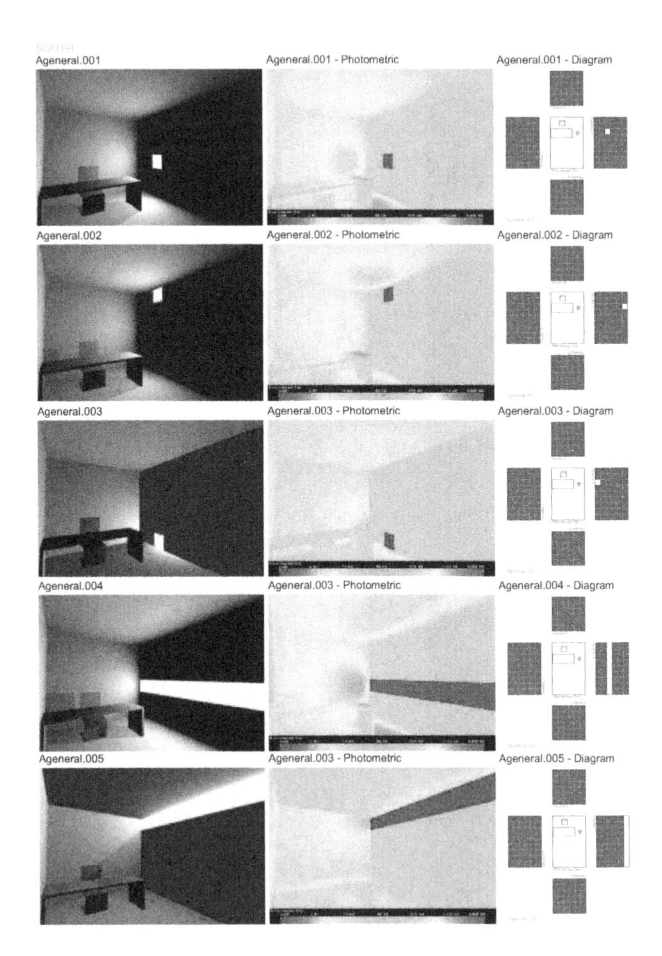

Experiments	Variables											
	Room Size	Room Shape	Surface Reflectance	Number of Sources of Luminance	Location of Sources of Luminance	Luminance of the entry field of view **(X and Y Axis)**	Luminance of the entry field of view **(Z axis)**	Observer Location and Line of Sight	Size of Aperture	Frequency of Luminaires	Contrast	Color of Surfaces
Three D Model South				IL					IL			

Color Key	
	Significant
	Less Significant
	Not Significant
IL	Influential Learning

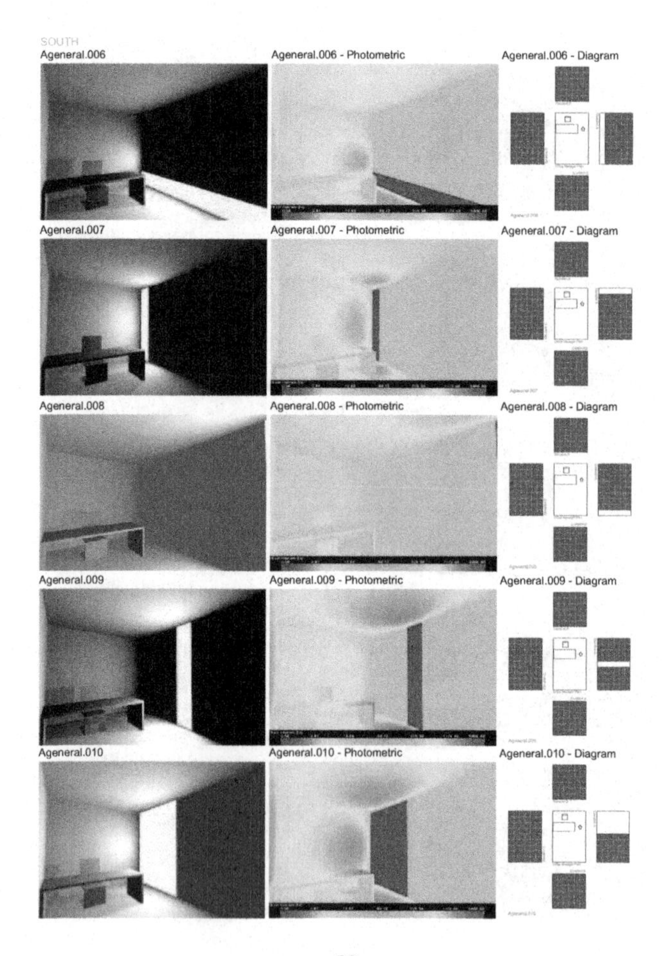

Experiments	Variables											
	Room Size	Room Shape	Surface Reflectance	Number of Sources of Luminance	Location of Sources of Luminance	Luminance of the entry field of view **(X and Y Axis)**	Luminance of the entry field of view **(Z axis)**	Observer Location and Line of Sight	Size of Aperture	Frequency of Luminaires	Contrast	Color of Surfaces
Three D Model East				IL					IL			

Color Key	
	Significant
	Less Significant
	Not Significant
IL	Influential Learning

EAST

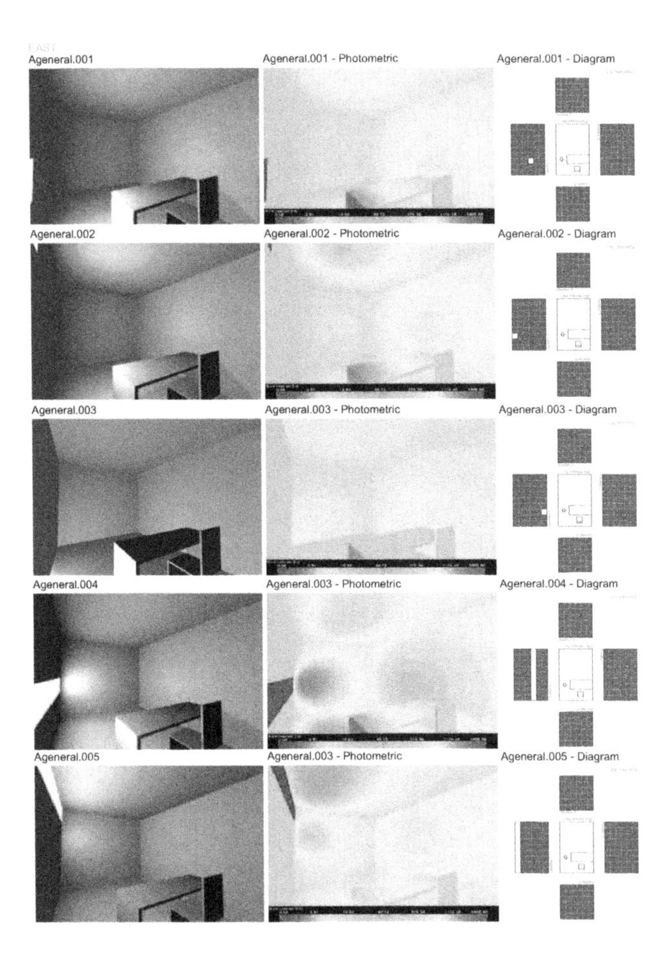

Experiments	Variables											
	Room Size	Room Shape	Surface Reflectance	Number of Sources of Luminance	Location of Sources of Luminance	Luminance of the entry field of view **(X and Y Axis)**	Luminance of the entry field of view **(Z axis)**	Observer Location and Line of Sight	Size of Aperture	Frequency of Luminaires	Contrast	Color of Surfaces
Three D Model East				IL					IL			

Color Key	
	Significant
	Less Significant
	Not Significant
IL	Influential Learning

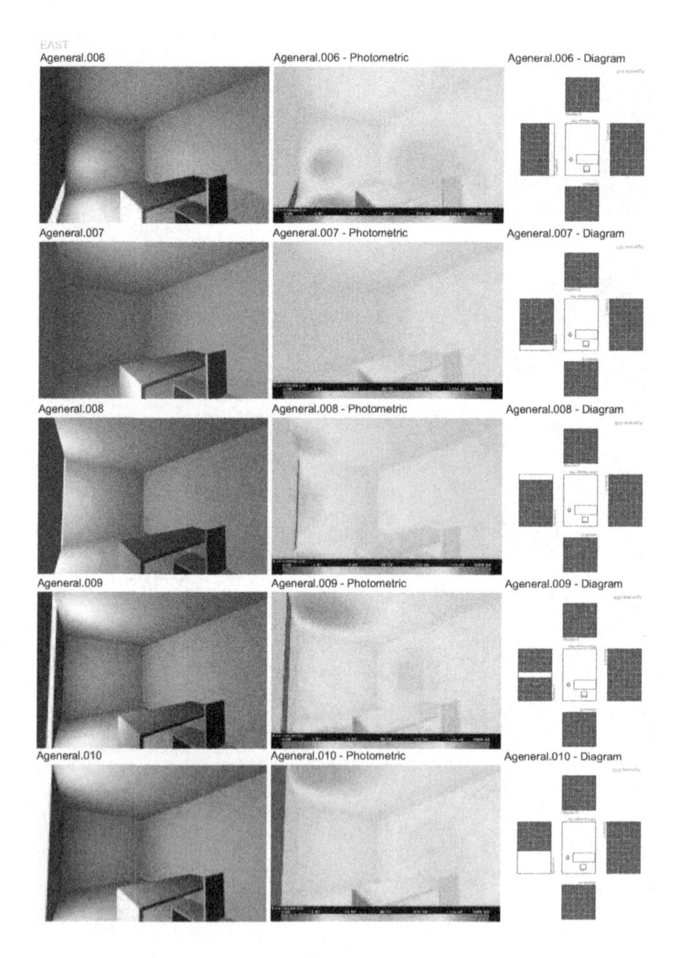

Experiments	Variables											
	Room Size	Room Shape	Surface Reflectance	Number of Sources of Luminance	Location of Sources of Luminance	Luminance of the entry field of view **(X and Y Axis)**	Luminance of the entry field of view **(Z axis)**	Observer Location and Line of Sight	Size of Aperture	Frequency of Luminaires	Contrast	Color of Surfaces
Three D Model West				IL					IL			

Color Key	
	Significant
	Less Significant
	Not Significant
IL	Influential Learning

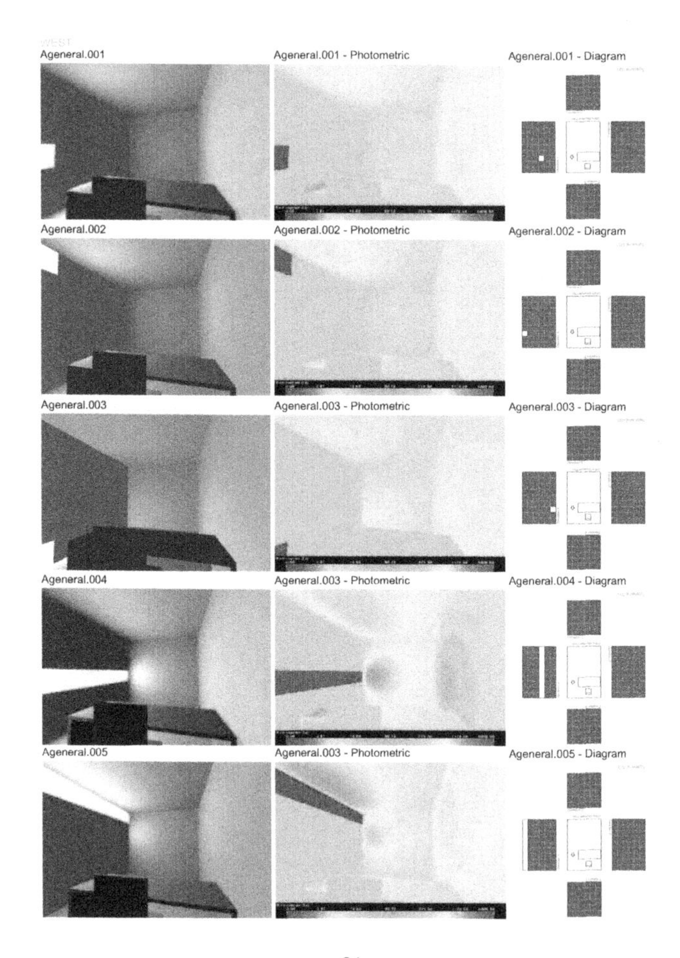

Experiments	Variables											
	Room Size	Room Shape	Surface Reflectance	Number of Sources of Luminance	Location of Sources of Luminance	Luminance of the entry field of view **(X and Y Axis)**	Luminance of the entry field of view **(Z axis)**	Observer Location and Line of Sight	Size of Aperture	Frequency of Luminaires	Contrast	Color of Surfaces
Three D Model West				IL					IL			

Color Key	
	Significant
	Less Significant
	Not Significant
IL	Influential Learning

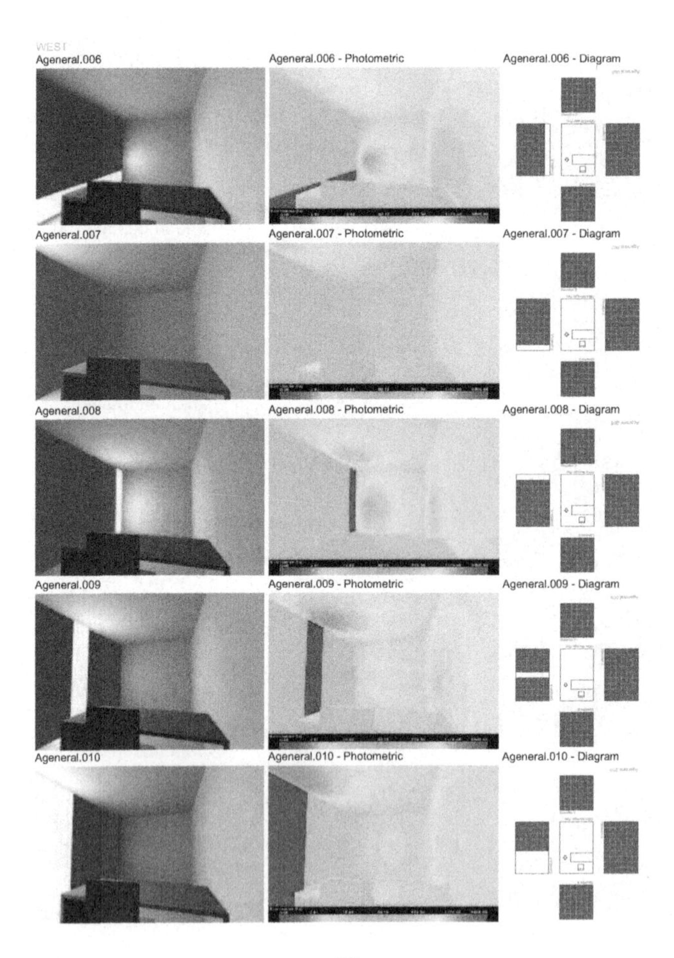

Experiments	Variables											
	Room Size	Room Shape	Surface Reflectance	Number of Sources of Luminance	Location of Sources of Luminance	Luminance of the entry field of view **(X and Y Axis)**	Luminance of the entry field of view **(Z axis)**	Observer Location and Line of Sight	Size of Aperture	Frequency of Luminaires	Contrast	Color of Surfaces
Three D Model North				IL					IL			

Color Key	
	Significant
	Less Significant
	Not Significant
IL	Influential Learning

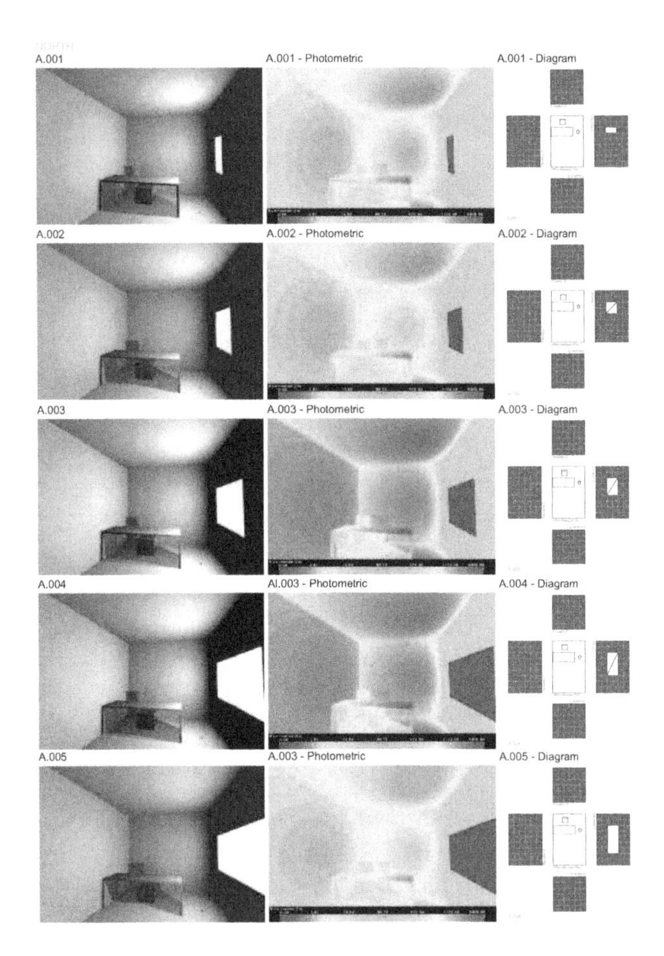

Experiments	Variables											
	Room Size	Room Shape	Surface Reflectance	Number of Sources of Luminance	Location of Sources of Luminance	Luminance of the entry field of view **(X and Y Axis)**	Luminance of the entry field of view **(Z axis)**	Observer Location and Line of Sight	Size of Aperture	Frequency of Luminaires	Contrast	Color of Surfaces
Three D Model North				IL					IL			

Color Key	
	Significant
	Less Significant
	Not Significant
IL	Influential Learning

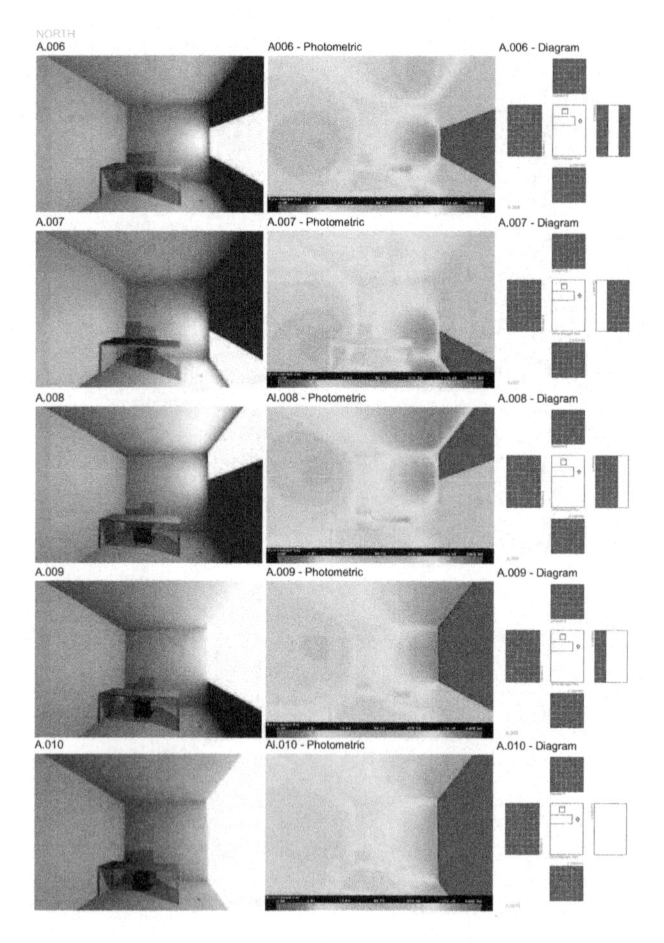

Experiments	Variables												
	Room Size	Room Shape	Surface Reflectance	Number of Sources of Luminance	Location of Sources of Luminance	Luminance of the entry field of view **(X and Y Axis)**	Luminance of the entry field of view **(Z axis)**	Observer Location and Line of Sight	Size of Aperture	Frequency of Luminaires	Contrast	Color of Surfaces
Three D Model South				IL					IL			

Color Key	
	Significant
	Less Significant
	Not Significant
IL	Influential Learning

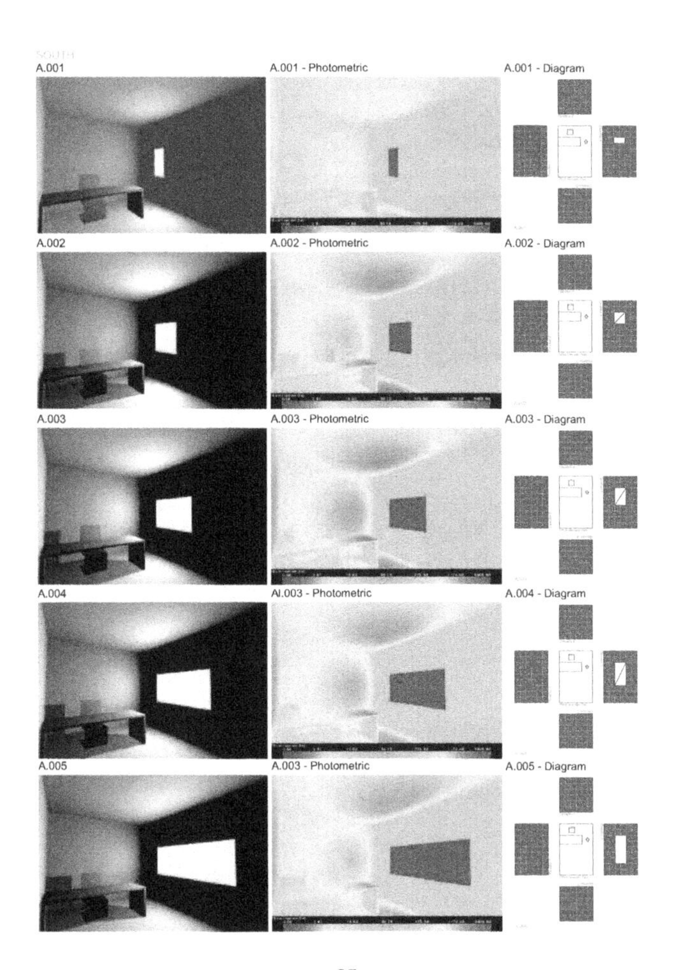

Experiments	Variables											
	Room Size	*Room Shape*	*Surface Reflectance*	*Number of Sources of Luminance*	*Location of Sources of Luminance*	*Luminance of the entry field of view* ***(X and Y Axis)***	*Luminance of the entry field of view* ***(Z axis)***	*Observer Location and Line of Sight*	*Size of Aperture*	*Frequency of Luminaires*	*Contrast*	*Color of Surfaces*
Three D Model South				IL					IL			

Color Key	
	Significant
	Less Significant
	Not Significant
IL	Influential Learning

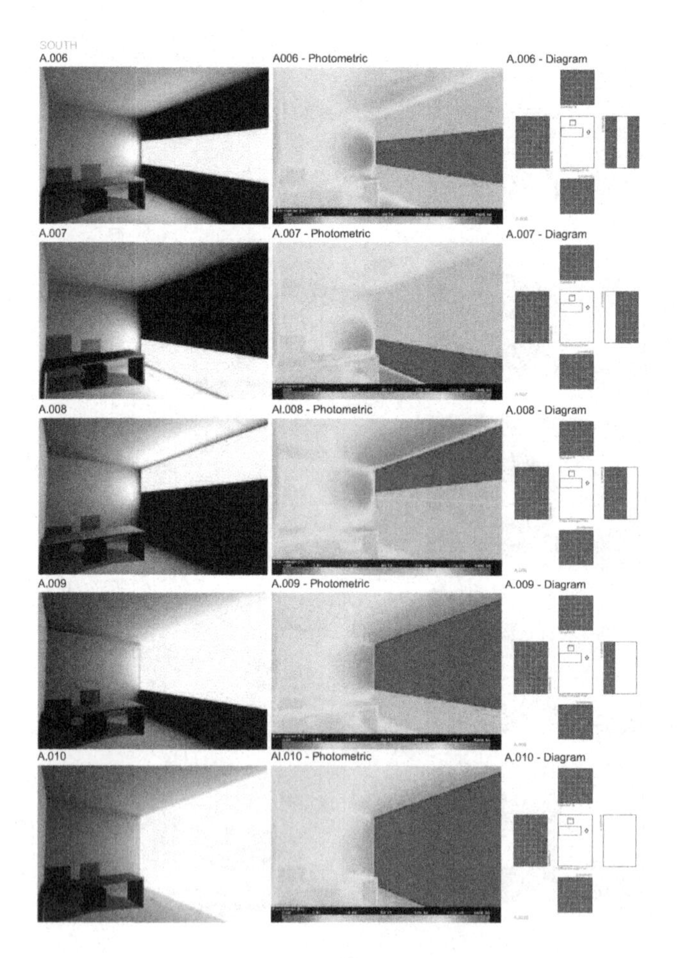

Experiments	Variables											
	Room Size	Room Shape	Surface Reflectance	Number of Sources of Luminance	Location of Sources of Luminance	Luminance of the entry field of view **(X and Y Axis)**	Luminance of the entry field of view **(Z axis)**	Observer Location and Line of Sight	Size of Aperture	Frequency of Luminaires	Contrast	Color of Surfaces
Three D Model East				IL					IL			

Color Key	
	Significant
	Less Significant
	Not Significant
IL	Influential Learning

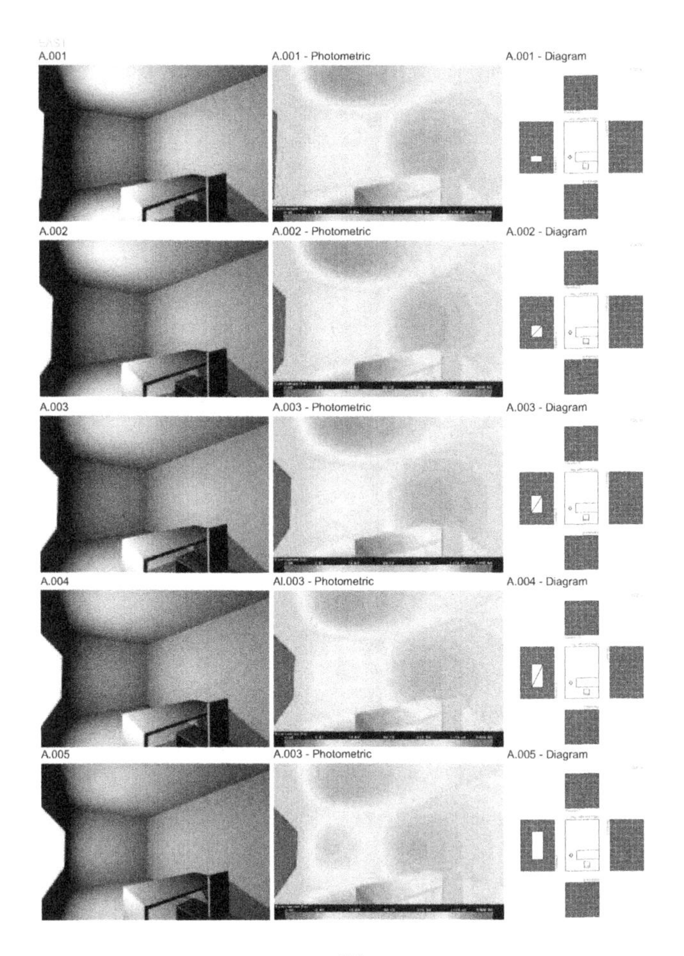

Experiments	Variables											
	Room Size	Room Shape	Surface Reflectance	Number of Sources of Luminance	Location of Sources of Luminance	Luminance of the entry field of view **(X and Y Axis)**	Luminance of the entry field of view **(Z axis)**	Observer Location and Line of Sight	Size of Aperture	Frequency of Luminaires	Contrast	Color of Surfaces
Three D Model East				IL					IL			

Color Key	
	Signficant
	Less Significant
	Not Significant
IL	Influential Learning

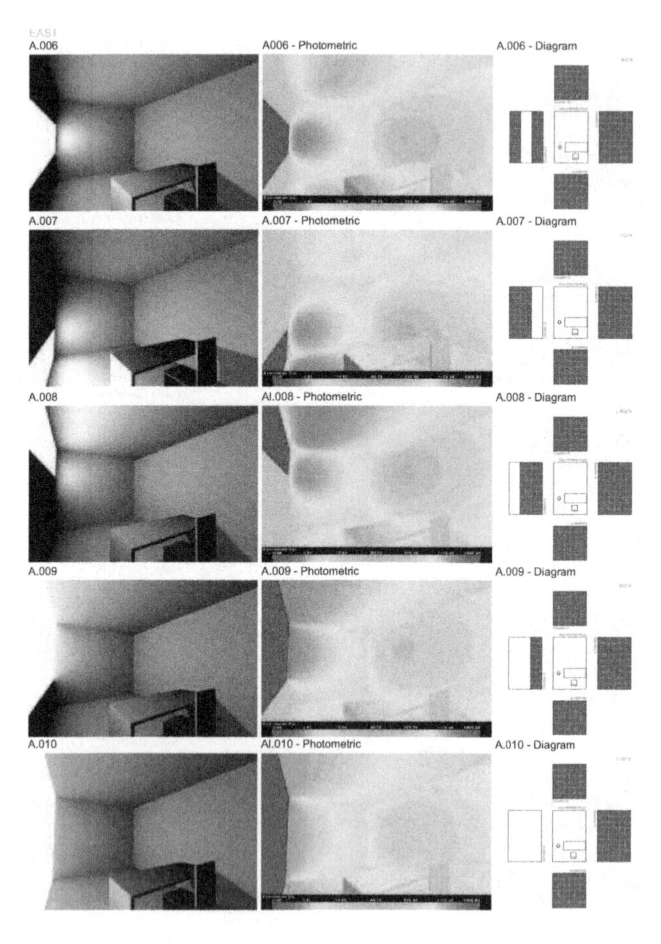

Experiments	Variables											
	Room Size	Room Shape	Surface Reflectance	Number of Sources of Luminance	Location of Sources of Luminance	Luminance of the entry field of view **(X and Y Axis)**	Luminance of the entry field of view **(Z axis)**	Observer Location and Line of Sight	Size of Aperture	Frequency of Luminaires	Contrast	Color of Surfaces
Three D Model West				IL					IL			

Color Key	
	Significant
	Less Significant
	Not Significant
IL	Influential Learning

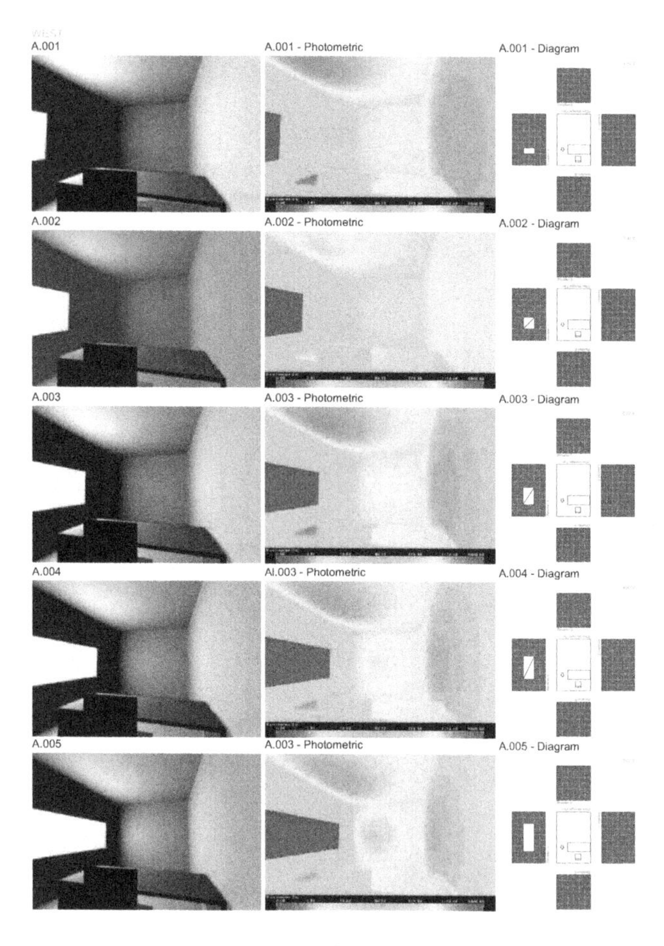

Experiments	Variables											
	Room Size	Room Shape	Surface Reflectance	Number of Sources of Luminance	Location of Sources of Luminance	Luminance of the entry field of view **(X and Y Axis)**	Luminance of the entry field of view **(Z axis)**	Observer Location and Line of Sight	Size of Aperture	Frequency of Luminaires	Contrast	Color of Surfaces
Three D Model West				IL					IL			

Color Key	
	Significant
	Less Significant
	Not Significant
IL	Influential Learning

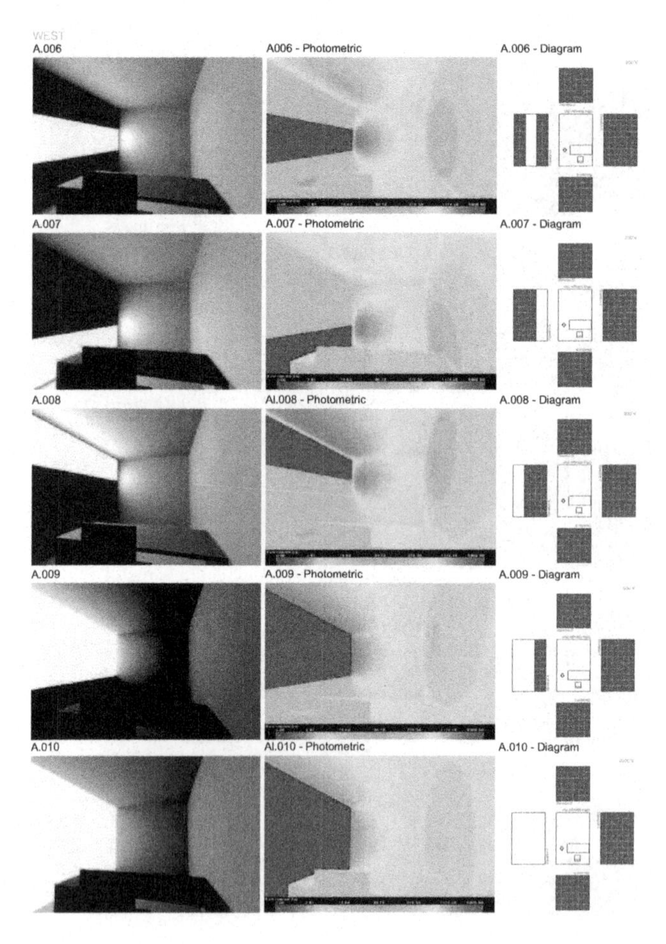

Experiments	Variables												
	Room Size	Room Shape	Surface Reflectance	Number of Sources of Luminance	Location of Sources of Luminance	Luminance of the entry field of view **(X and Y Axis)**	Luminance of the entry field of view **(Z axis)**	Observer Location and Line of Sight	Size of Aperture	Frequency of Luminaires	Contrast	Color of Surfaces
Three D Model North				IL					IL			

Color Key	
	Significant
	Less Significant
	Not Significant
IL	Influential Learning

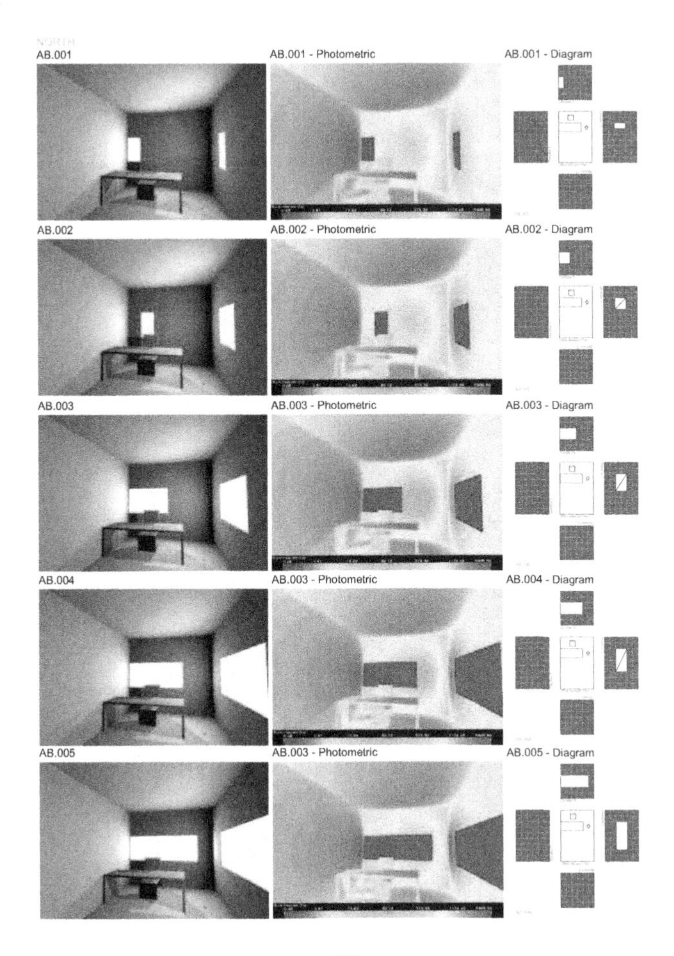

Experiments	Variables											
	Room Size	Room Shape	Surface Reflectance	Number of Sources of Luminance	Location of Sources of Luminance	Luminance of the entry field of view **(X and Y Axis)**	Luminance of the entry field of view **(Z axis)**	Observer Location and Line of Sight	Size of Aperture	Frequency of Luminaires	Contrast	Color of Surfaces
Three D Model North				IL					IL			

Color Key	
	Significant
	Less Significant
	Not Significant
IL	Influential Learning

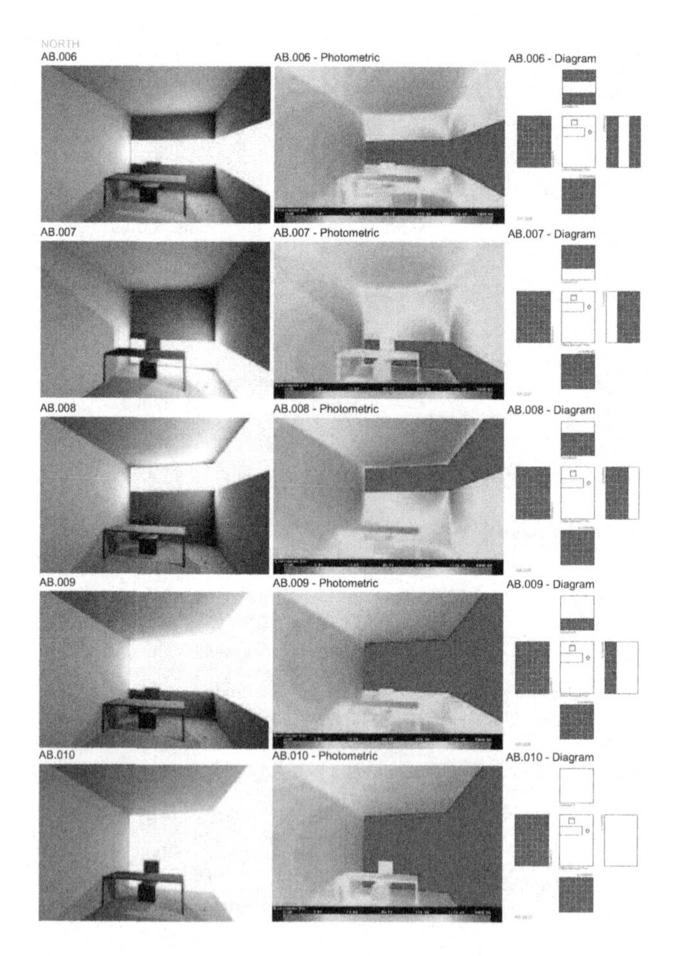

Experiments	Variables											
	Room Size	Room Shape	Surface Reflectance	Number of Sources of Luminance	Location of Sources of Luminance	Luminance of the entry field of view **(X and Y Axis)**	Luminance of the entry field of view **(Z axis)**	Observer Location and Line of Sight	Size of Aperture	Frequency of Luminaires	Contrast	Color of Surfaces
Three D Model South				IL					IL			

Color Key	
	Significant
	Less Significant
	Not Significant
IL	Influential Learning

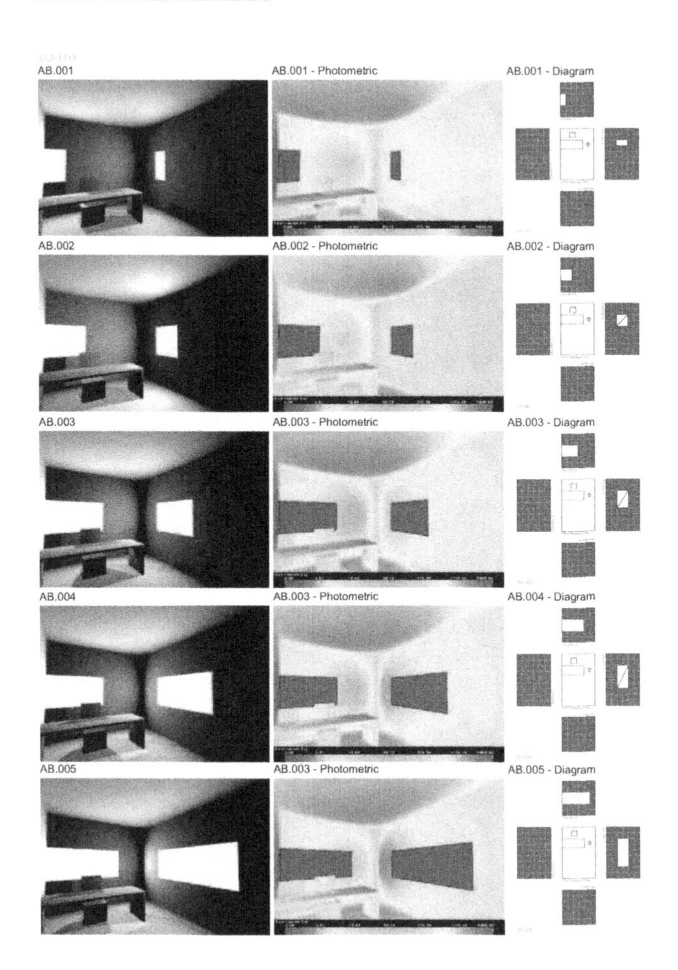

Experiments	Variables											
	Room Size	Room Shape	Surface Reflectance	Number of Sources of Luminance	Location of Sources of Luminance	Luminance of the entry field of view **(X and Y Axis)**	Luminance of the entry field of view **(Z axis)**	Observer Location and Line of Sight	Size of Aperture	Frequency of Luminaires	Contrast	Color of Surfaces
Three D Model South				IL					IL			

Color Key	
	Significant
	Less Significant
	Not Significant
IL	Influential Learning

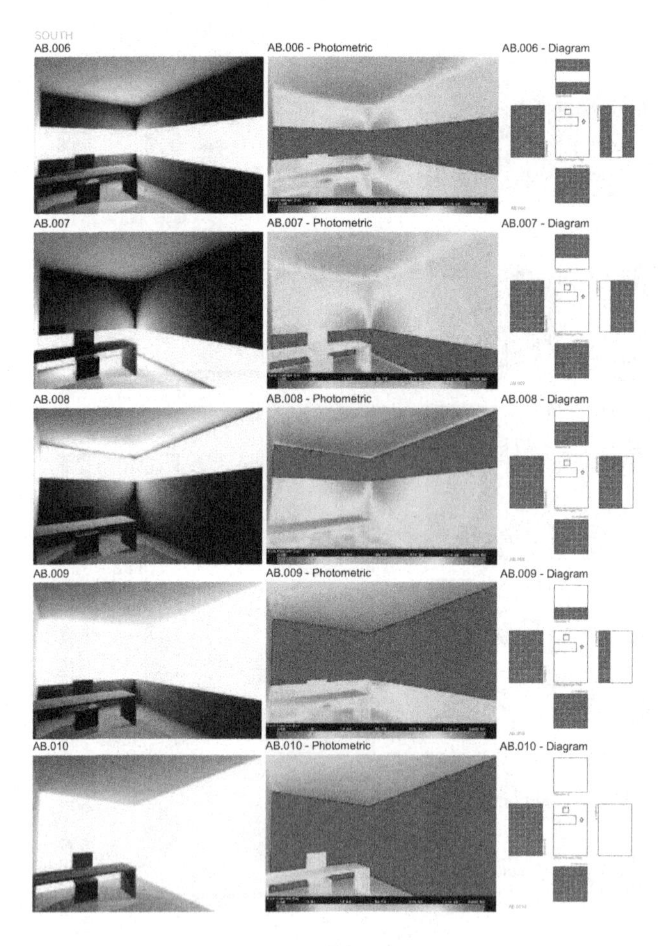

Experiments	Variables											
	Room Size	Room Shape	Surface Reflectance	Number of Sources of Luminance	Location of Sources of Luminance	Luminance of the entry field of view **(X and Y Axis)**	Luminance of the entry field of view **(Z axis)**	Observer Location and Line of Sight	Size of Aperture	Frequency of Luminaires	Contrast	Color of Surfaces
Three D Model East				IL					IL			

Color Key	
	Significant
	Less Significant
	Not Significant
IL	Influential Learning

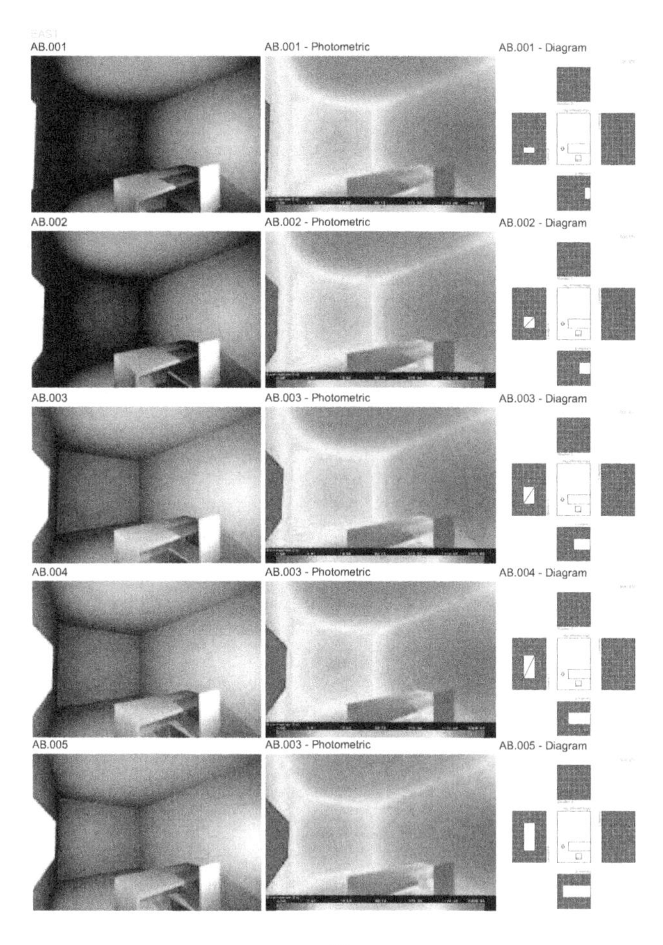

Experiments	Variables											
	Room Size	*Room Shape*	*Surface Reflectance*	*Number of Sources of Luminance*	*Location of Sources of Luminance*	*Luminance of the entry field of view* ***(X and Y Axis)***	*Luminance of the entry field of view* ***(Z axis)***	*Observer Location and Line of Sight*	*Size of Aperture*	*Frequency of Luminaires*	*Contrast*	*Color of Surfaces*
Three D Model East				IL					IL			

Color Key	
	Significant
	Less Significant
	Not Significant
IL	Influential Learning

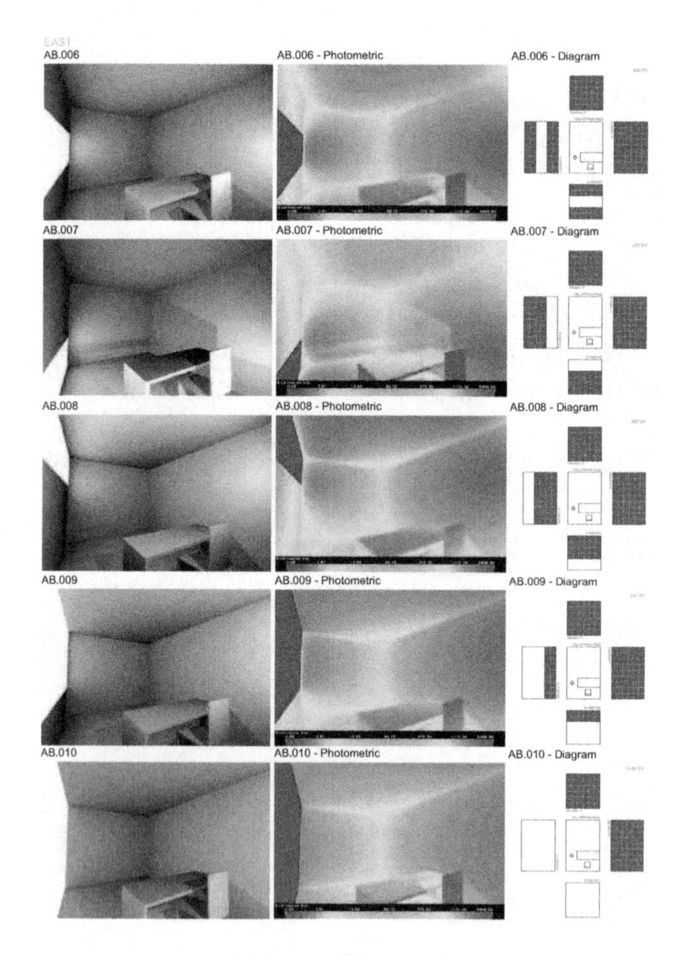

	Variables											
Experiments	Room Size	Room Shape	Surface Reflectance	Number of Sources of Luminance	Location of Sources of Luminance	Luminance of the entry field of view **(X and Y Axis)**	Luminance of the entry field of view **(Z axis)**	Observer Location and Line of Sight	Size of Aperture	Frequency of Luminaires	Contrast	Color of Surfaces
Three D Model West				IL					IL			

Color Key	
	Significant
	Less Significant
	Not Significant
IL	Influential Learning

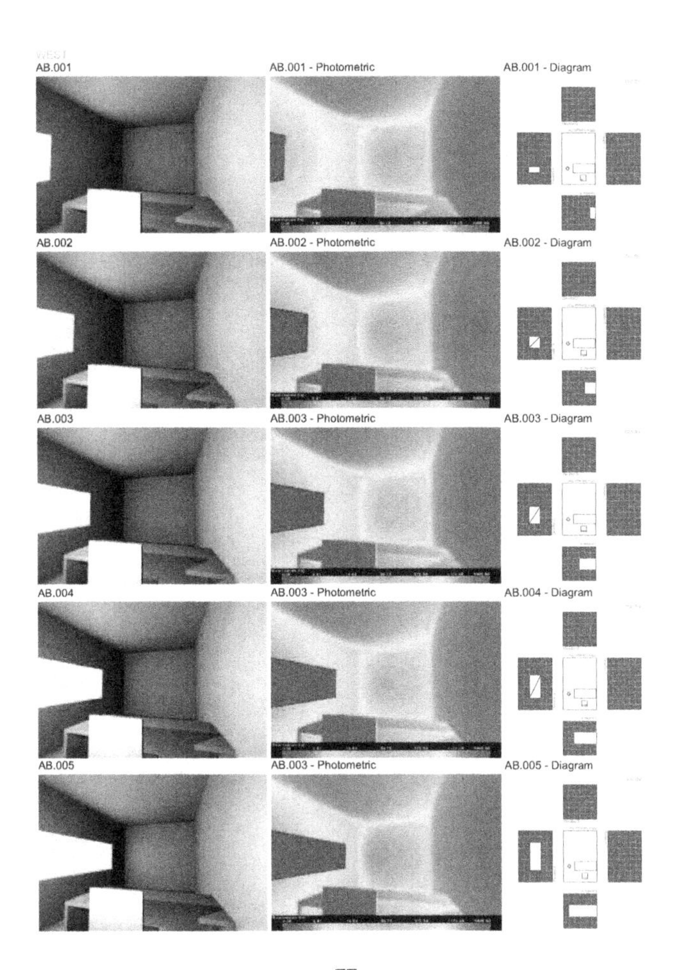

Experiments	Variables											
	Room Size	Room Shape	Surface Reflectance	Number of Sources of Luminance	Location of Sources of Luminance	Luminance of the entry field of view **(X and Y Axis)**	Luminance of the entry field of view **(Z axis)**	Observer Location and Line of Sight	Size of Aperture	Frequency of Luminaires	Contrast	Color of Surfaces
Three D Model West				IL					IL			

Color Key	
	Signficant
	Less Significant
	Not Significant
IL	Influential Learning

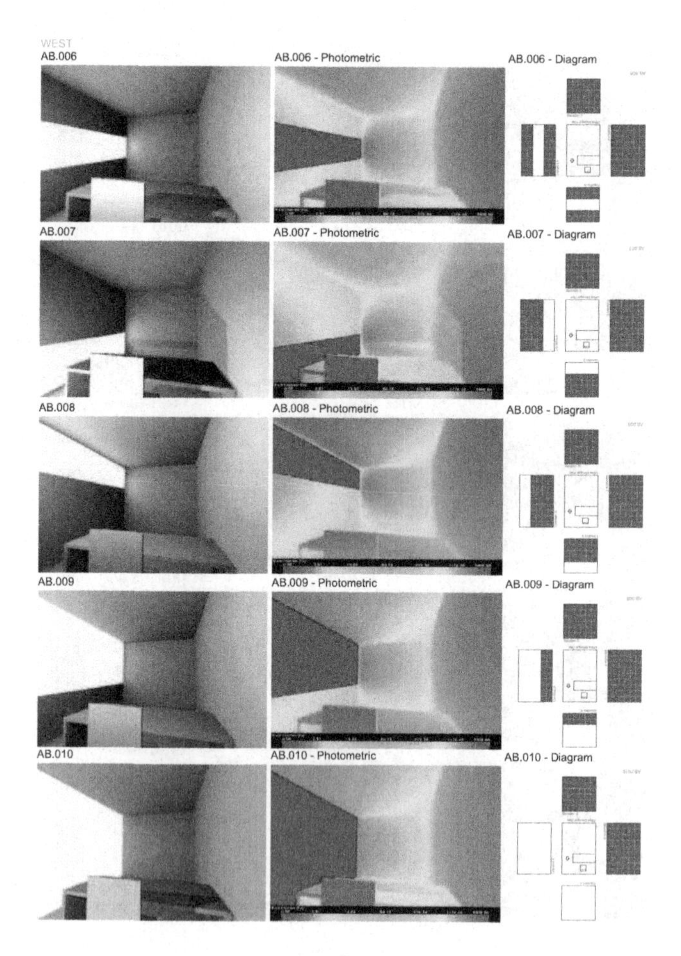

Experiments	Variables											
	Room Size	Room Shape	Surface Reflectance	Number of Sources of Luminance	Location of Sources of Luminance	Luminance of the entry field of view **(X and Y Axis)**	Luminance of the entry field of view **(Z axis)**	Observer Location and Line of Sight	Size of Aperture	Frequency of Luminaires	Contrast	Color of Surfaces
Three D Model North				IL					IL			

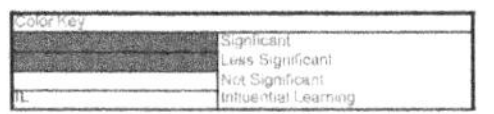

Color Key	
	Significant
	Less Significant
	Not Significant
IL	Influential Learning

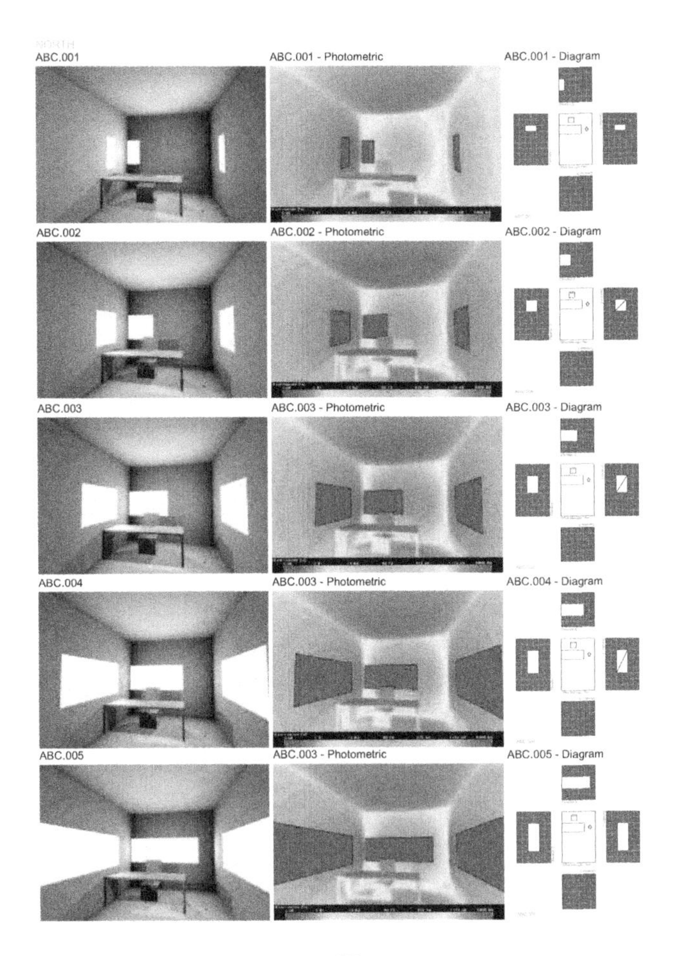

Experiments	Variables											
	Room Size	Room Shape	Surface Reflectance	Number of Sources of Luminance	Location of Sources of Luminance	Luminance of the entry field of view **(X and Y Axis)**	Luminance of the entry field of view **(Z axis)**	Observer Location and Line of Sight	Size of Aperture	Frequency of Luminaires	Contrast	Color of Surfaces
Three D Model North				IL					IL			

Color Key	
	Significant
	Less Significant
	Not Significant
IL	Influential Learning

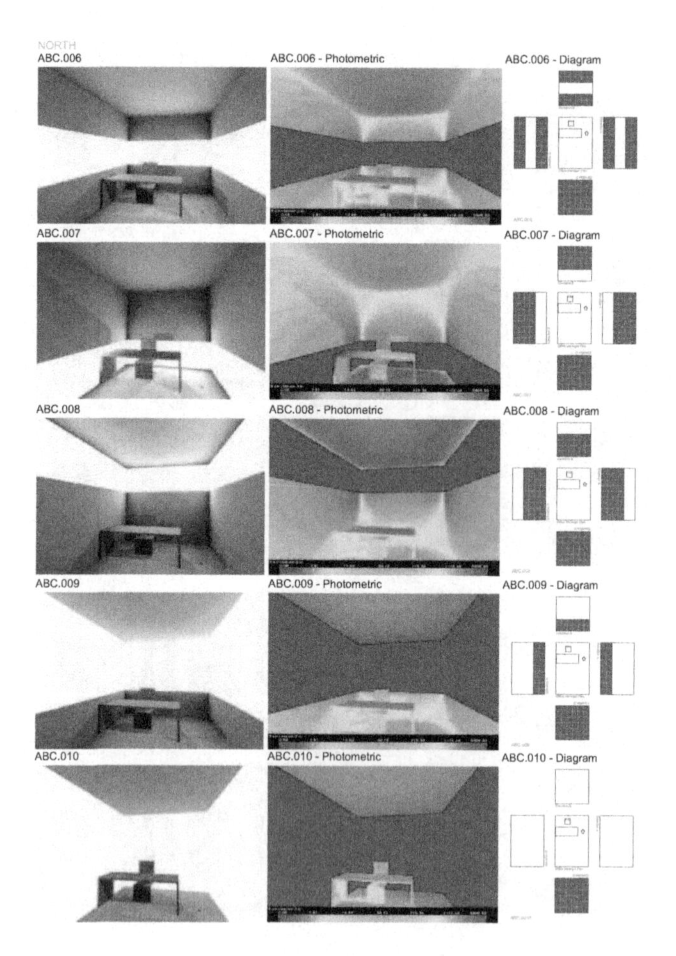

	Variables											
Experiments	Room Size	Room Shape	Surface Reflectance	Number of Sources of Luminance	Location of Sources of Luminance	Luminance of the entry field of view **(X and Y Axis)**	Luminance of the entry field of view **(Z axis)**	Observer Location and Line of Sight	Size of Aperture	Frequency of Luminaires	Contrast	Color of Surfaces
Three D Model North				IL					IL			

Color Key	
	Significant
	Less Significant
	Not Significant
IL	Influential Learning

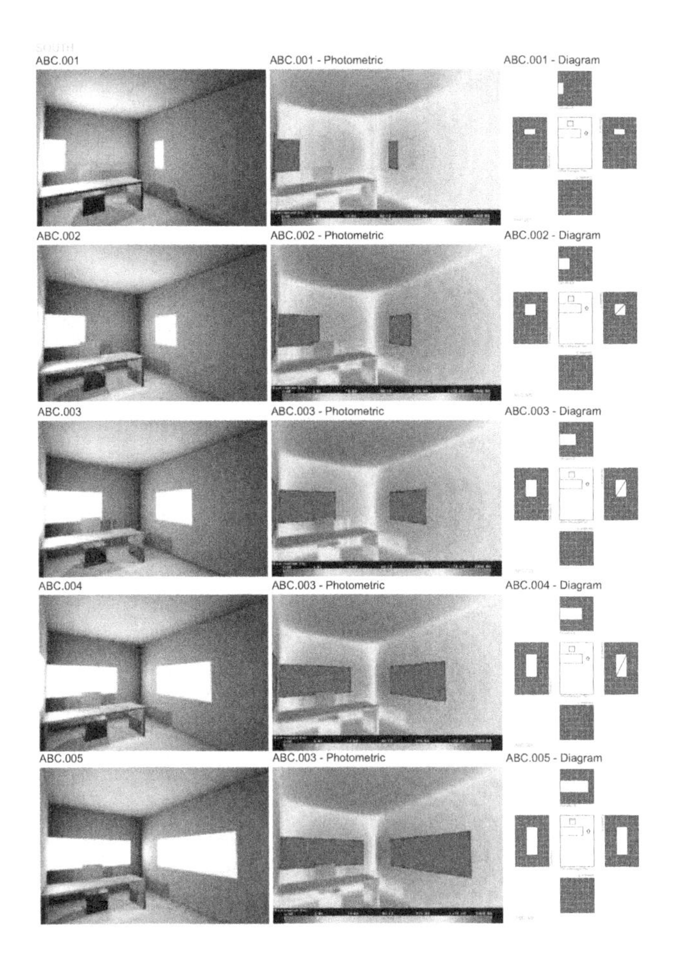

Experiments	Variables											
	Room Size	Room Shape	Surface Reflectance	Number of Sources of Luminance	Location of Sources of Luminance	Luminance of the entry field of view **(X and Y Axis)**	Luminance of the entry field of view **(Z axis)**	Observer Location and Line of Sight	Size of Aperture	Frequency of Luminaires	Contrast	Color of Surfaces
Three D Model North				IL					IL			

Color Key	
	Significant
	Less Significant
	Not Significant
IL	Influential Learning

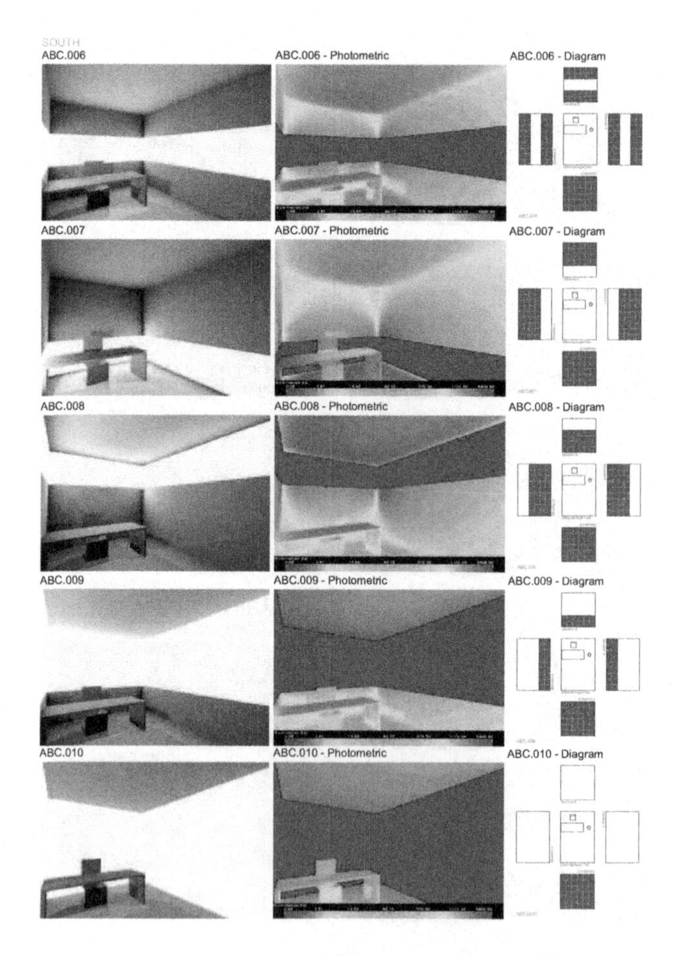

Experiments	Variables											
	Room Size	Room Shape	Surface Reflectance	Number of Sources of Luminance	Location of Sources of Luminance	Luminance of the entry field of view ***(X and Y Axis)***	Luminance of the entry field of view ***(Z axis)***	Observer Location and Line of Sight	Size of Aperture	Frequency of Luminaires	Contrast	Color of Surfaces
Three D Model North				IL					IL			

Color Key	
	Significant
	Less Significant
	Not Significant
IL	Influential Learning

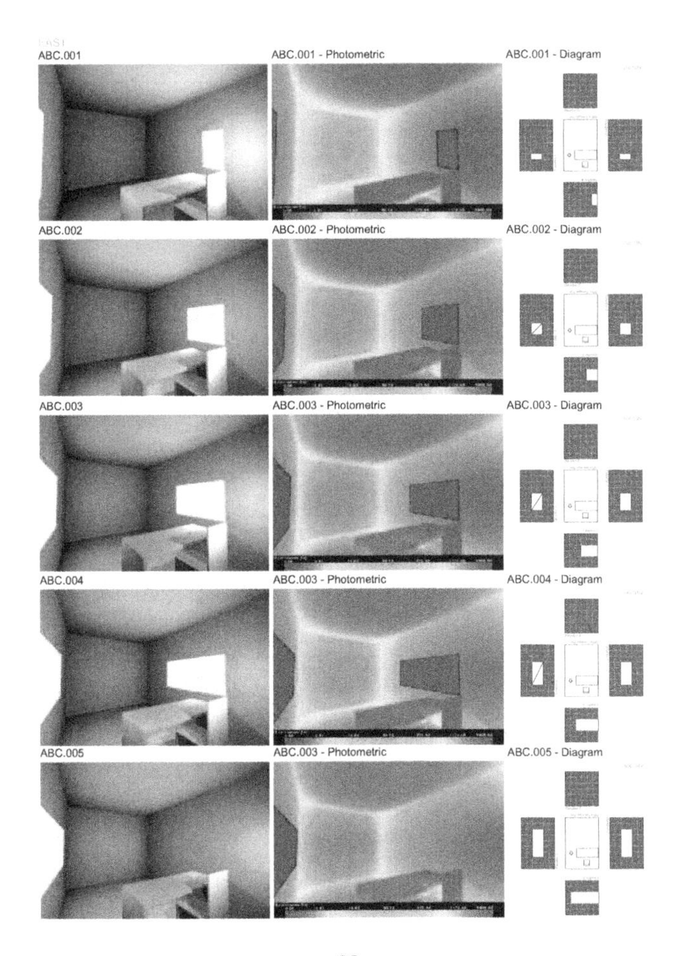

Experiments	Variables											
	Room Size	Room Shape	Surface Reflectance	Number of Sources of Luminance	Location of Sources of Luminance	Luminance of the entry field of view **(X and Y Axis)**	Luminance of the entry field of view **(Z axis)**	Observer Location and Line of Sight	Size of Aperture	Frequency of Luminaires	Contrast	Color of Surfaces
Three D Model North				IL					IL			

Color Key	
	Signficant
	Less Significant
	Not Significant
IL	Influential Learning

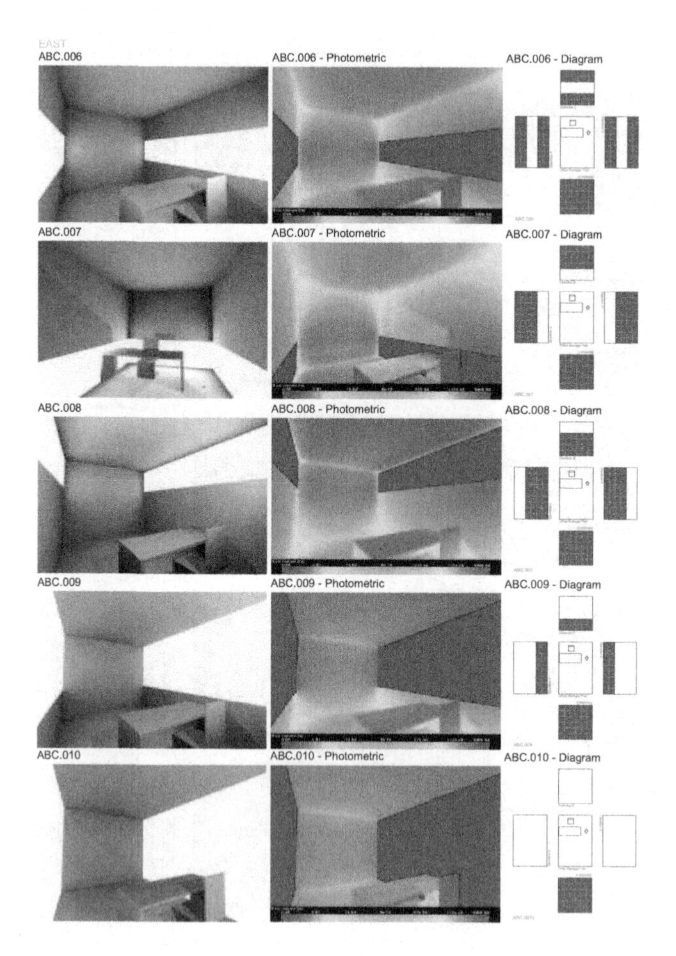

Experiments	Variables											
	Room Size	Room Shape	Surface Reflectance	Number of Sources of Luminance	Location of Sources of Luminance	Luminance of the entry field of view **(X and Y Axis)**	Luminance of the entry field of view **(Z axis)**	Observer Location and Line of Sight	Size of Aperture	Frequency of Luminaires	Contrast	Color of Surfaces
Three D Model North				IL					IL			

Color Key	
	Significant
	Less Significant
	Not Significant
IL	Influential Learning

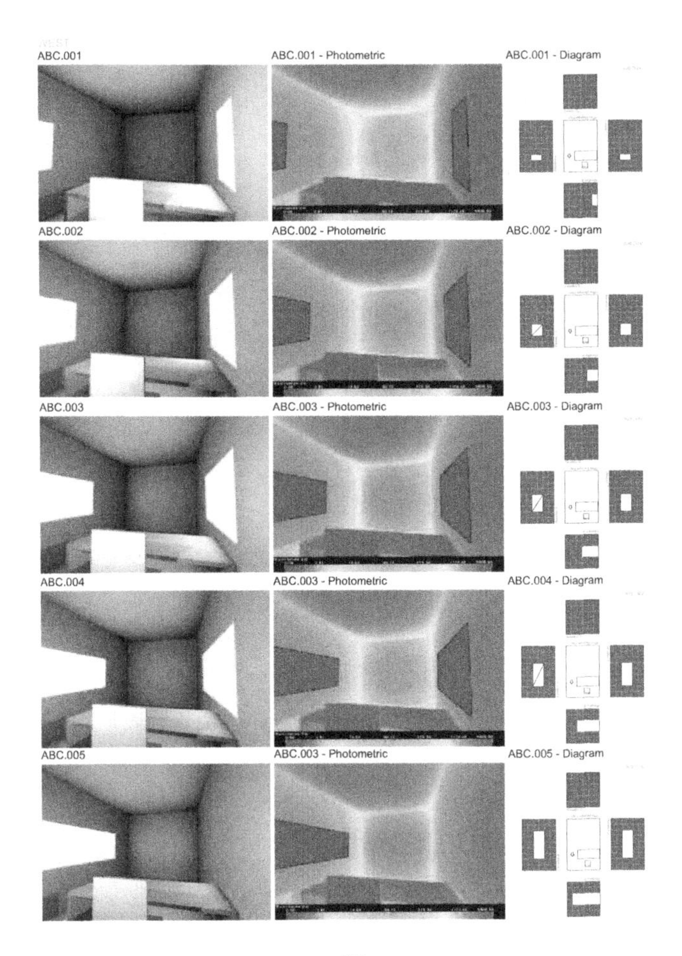

Experiments	Variables											
	Room Size	Room Shape	Surface Reflectance	Number of Sources of Luminance	Location of Sources of Luminance	Luminance of the entry field of view **(X and Y Axis)**	Luminance of the entry field of view **(Z axis)**	Observer Location and Line of Sight	Size of Aperture	Frequency of Luminaires	Contrast	Color of Surfaces
Three D Model North				IL					IL			

Color Key	
	Significant
	Less Significant
	Not Significant
IL	Influential Learning

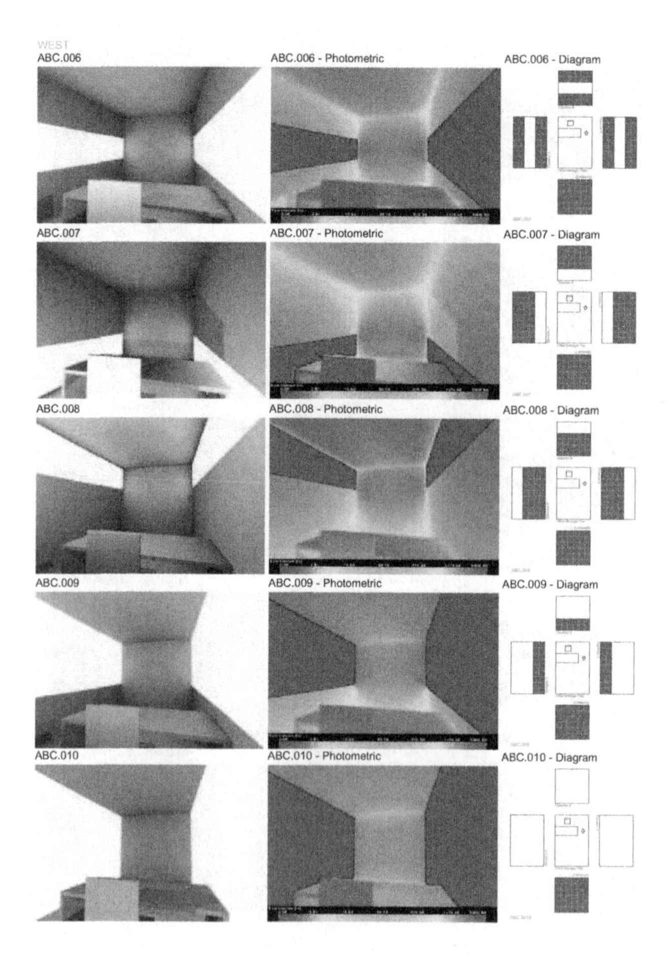

	Variables											
Experiments	Room Size	Room Shape	Surface Reflectance	Number of Sources of Luminance	Location of Sources of Luminance	Luminance of the entry field of view **(X and Y Axis)**	Luminance of the entry field of view **(Z axis)**	Observer Location and Line of Sight	Size of Aperture	Frequency of Luminaires	Contrast	Color of Surfaces
Three D Model North				IL					IL			

Color Key	
	Significant
	Less Significant
	Not Significant
IL	Influential Learning

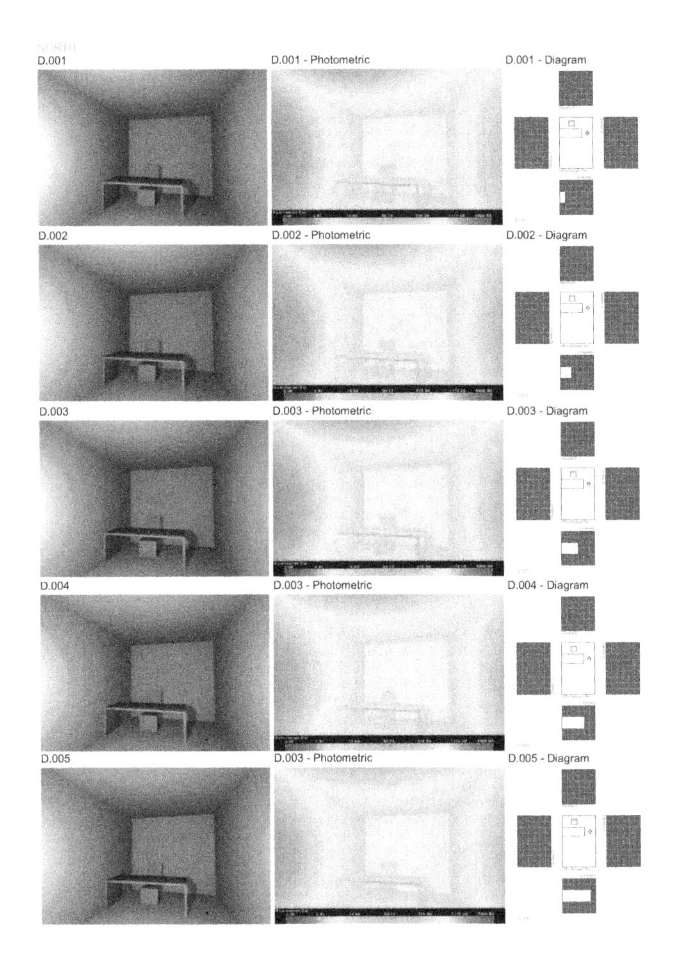

Experiments	Variables											
	Room Size	Room Shape	Surface Reflectance	Number of Sources of Luminance	Location of Sources of Luminance	Luminance of the entry field of view **(X and Y Axis)**	Luminance of the entry field of view **(Z axis)**	Observer Location and Line of Sight	Size of Aperture	Frequency of Luminaires	Contrast	Color of Surfaces
Three D Model North				IL					IL			

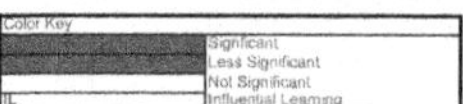

Color Key	
	Significant
	Less Significant
	Not Significant
IL	Influential Learning

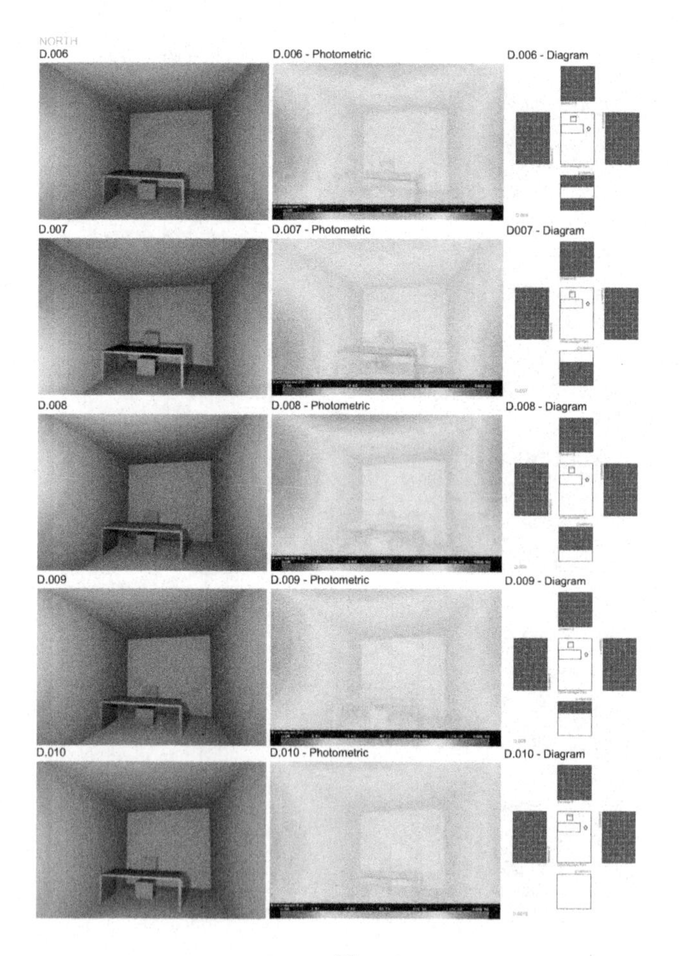

Experiments	Variables											
	Room Size	Room Shape	Surface Reflectance	Number of Sources of Luminance	Location of Sources of Luminance	Luminance of the entry field of view ***(X and Y Axis)***	Luminance of the entry field of view ***(Z axis)***	Observer Location and Line of Sight	Size of Aperture	Frequency of Luminaires	Contrast	Color of Surfaces
Three D Model South				IL					IL			

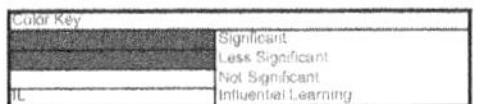

Color Key	
	Significant
	Less Significant
	Not Significant
IL	Influential Learning

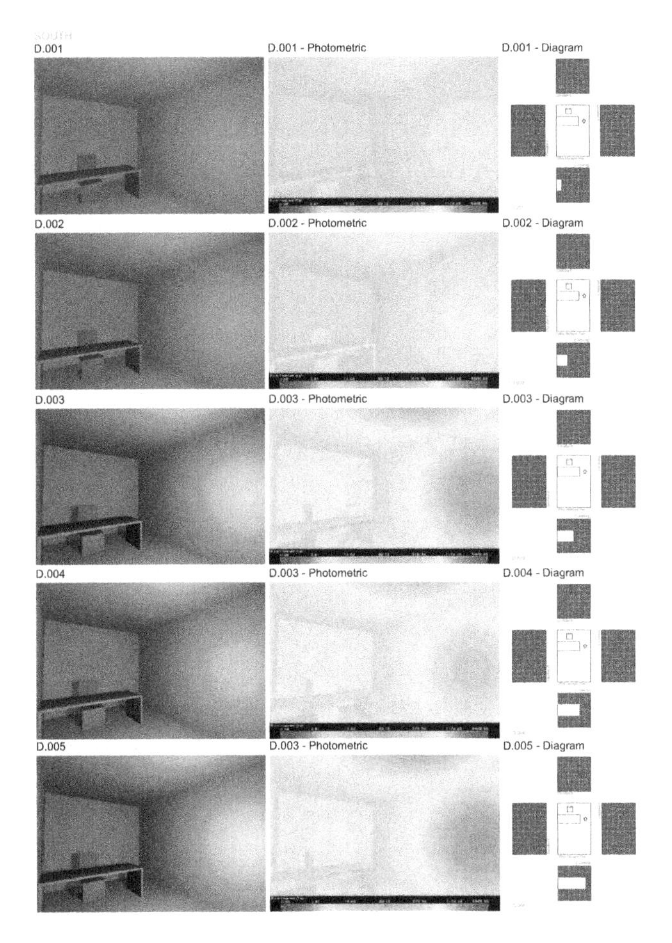

Experiments	Variables											
	Room Size	Room Shape	Surface Reflectance	Number of Sources of Luminance	Location of Sources of Luminance	Luminance of the entry field of view **(X and Y Axis)**	Luminance of the entry field of view **(Z axis)**	Observer Location and Line of Sight	Size of Aperture	Frequency of Luminaires	Contrast	Color of Surfaces
Three D Model South				IL					IL			

Color Key	
	Significant
	Less Significant
	Not Significant
IL	Influential Learning

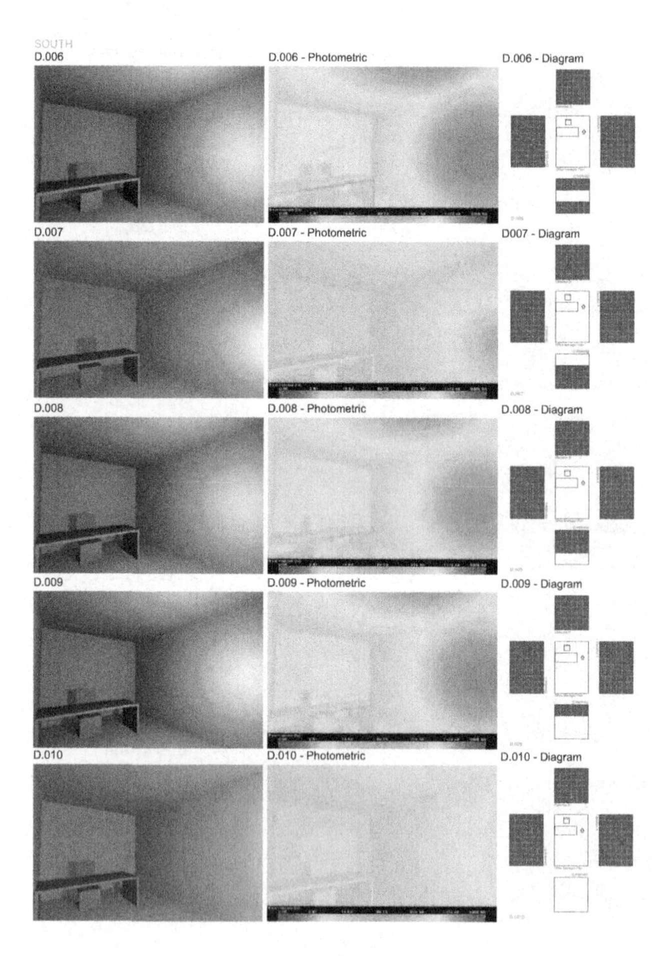

Experiments	Variables											
	Room Size	Room Shape	Surface Reflectance	Number of Sources of Luminance	Location of Sources of Luminance	Luminance of the entry field of view **(X and Y Axis)**	Luminance of the entry field of view **(Z axis)**	Observer Location and Line of Sight	Size of Aperture	Frequency of Luminaires	Contrast	Color of Surfaces
Three D Model East				IL					IL			

Color Key	
	Significant
	Less Significant
	Not Significant
IL	Influential Learning

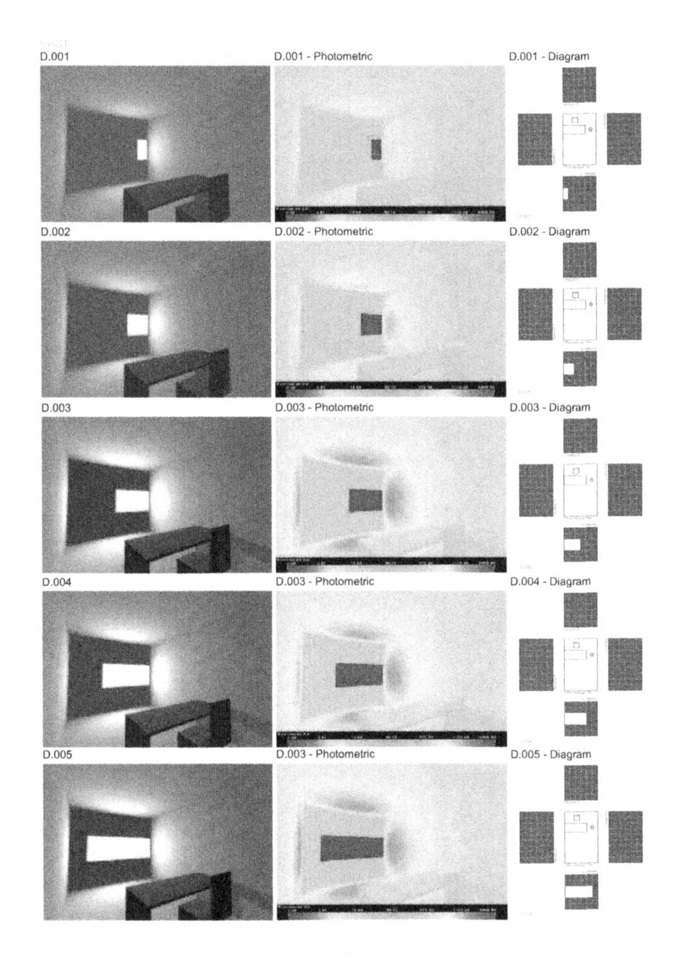

	Variables											
Experiments	Room Size	Room Shape	Surface Reflectance	Number of Sources of Luminance	Location of Sources of Luminance	Luminance of the entry field of view **(X and Y Axis)**	Luminance of the entry field of view **(Z axis)**	Observer Location and Line of Sight	Size of Aperture	Frequency of Luminaires	Contrast	Color of Surfaces
Three D Model East				IL					IL			

Color Key	
	Significant
	Less Significant
	Not Significant
IL	Influential Learning

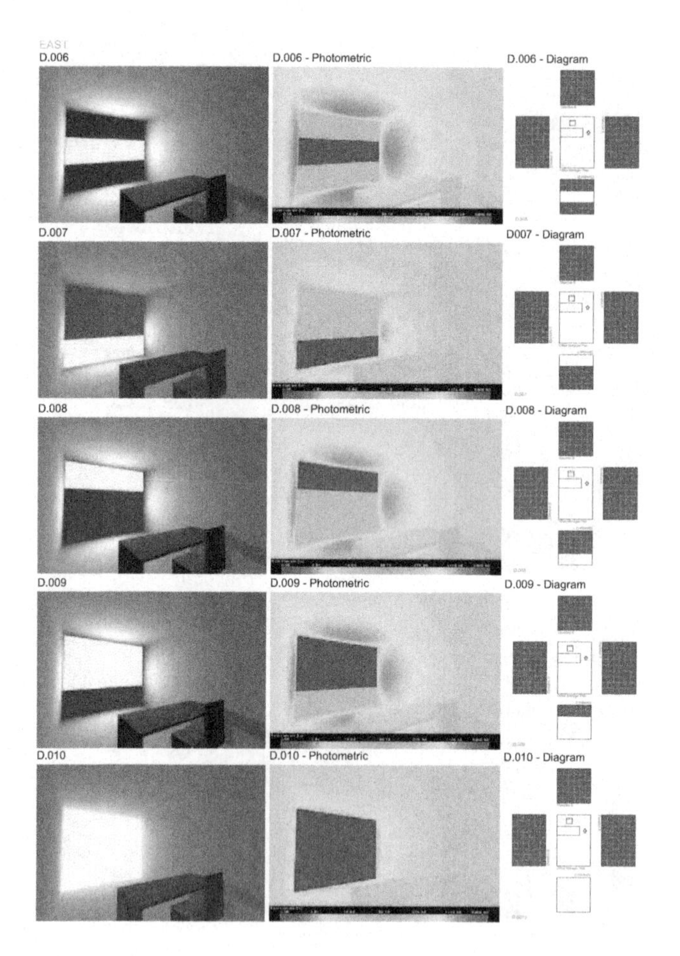

Experiments	Variables												
	Room Size	Room Shape	Surface Reflectance	Number of Sources of Luminance	Location of Sources of Luminance	Luminance of the entry field of view **(X and Y Axis)**	Luminance of the entry field of view **(Z axis)**	Observer Location and Line of Sight	Size of Aperture	Frequency of Luminaires	Contrast	Color of Surfaces
Three D Model West				IL					IL			

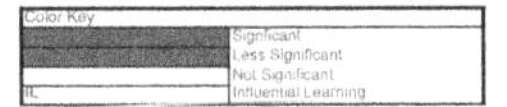

Color Key	
	Significant
	Less Significant
	Not Significant
IL	Influential Learning

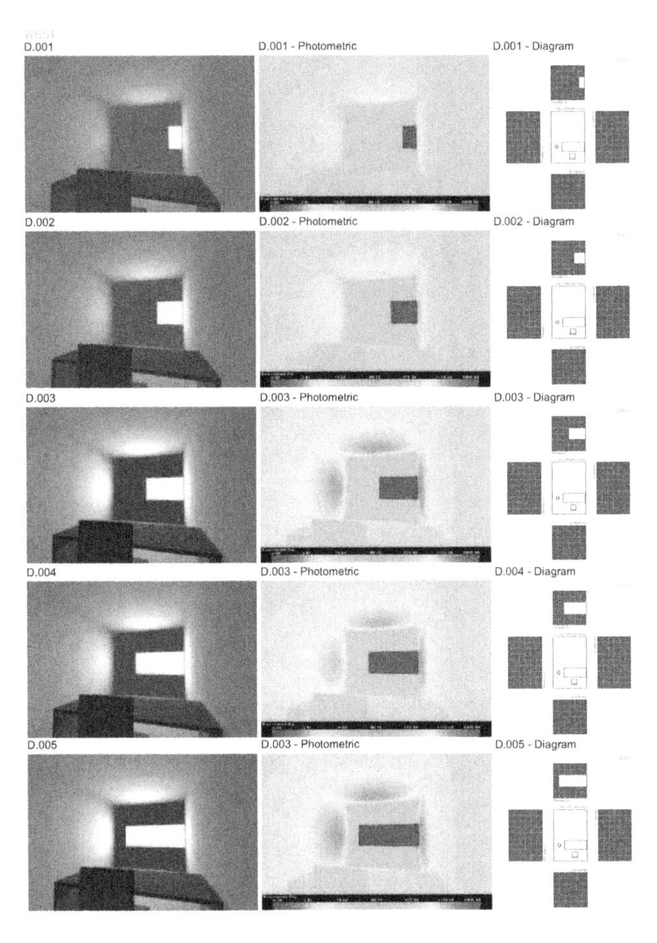

Experiments	Variables											
	Room Size	*Room Shape*	*Surface Reflectance*	*Number of Sources of Luminance*	*Location of Sources of Luminance*	*Luminance of the entry field of view* ***(X and Y Axis)***	*Luminance of the entry field of view* ***(Z axis)***	*Observer Location and Line of Sight*	*Size of Aperture*	*Frequency of Luminaires*	*Contrast*	*Color of Surfaces*
Three D Model West				IL					IL			

Color Key	
	Significant
	Less Significant
	Not Significant
IL	Influential Learning

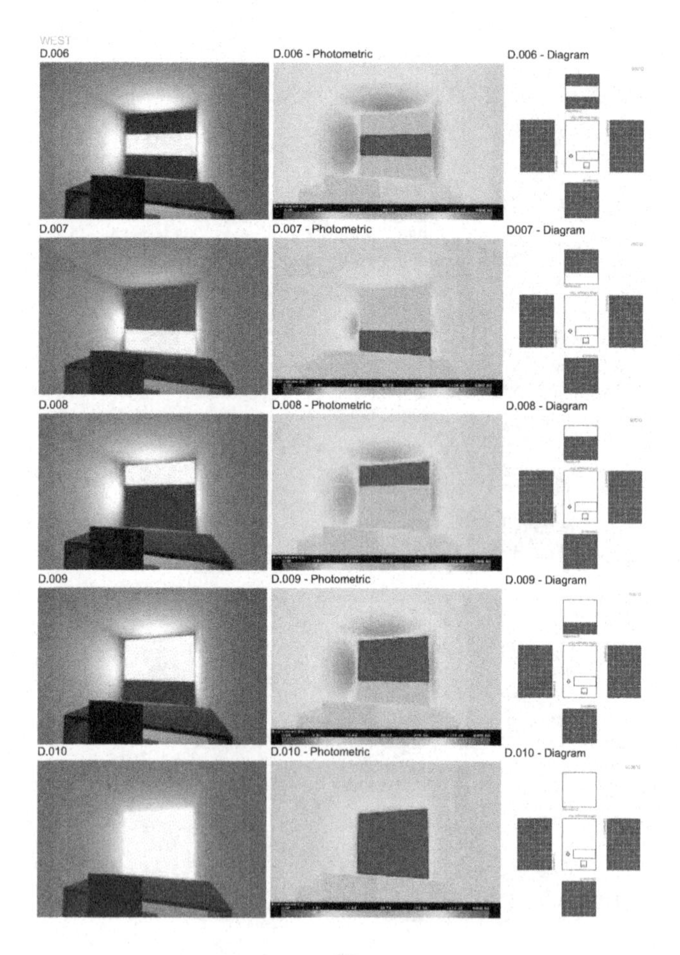

SECTION C: APPLIED RESEARCH IN DESIGN - INSITE EXPERIMENTS

In addition to the test facility and computer simulated models, the following experiments were also conducted:

Listing of Experiments:

- In Site Experiment A
- In Site Experiment C
- In Site Experiment D
- In Site Experiment E
- In Site Experiment F
- In Site Experiment G

INSITE EXPERIMENT A – BEACH HOUSE[1]

General Overview / Objective:

- To create a private internal space for the clients to 'party' and 'relax' on the weekend.
- Design a low budget, 'boys hangout', situated in the Southern part of Kuwait.
- Consists of 3 dorm-like bedrooms, with in suite bathrooms
- Includes common living space, kitchen and dining area
- Single story with roof terrace
- Faces the ocean on the East, and the desert on the West

Question: How do we increase the size of the windows (to extend the view of the exterior) while maintaining visual comfort?

Applicable Variables:

- Number of Sources of Luminance
- Location of Sources of Luminance
- **Observer Location of Line of Sight (IL)**
- Size of the Aperture

Influential Learning: Due to the internal courtyard design of the project and situating the windows strategically allowed the eyes to constantly have access to daylight which extended the view, enhancing stimulation of the eye.

A1, A2, A6 and A7

- Internal courtyard used to achieve maximum privacy for the end users.
- In parallel, maximum transparency was intended for purposes of viewing the most of the desert.

[1] First Building Designed by N. Abulhasan

- The main living space overlooks both the desert and the internal courtyard which are East-West oriented as seen in the exhibits.
- Multiple daylight sources through full height windows
- Due to the presence of the courtyard, daylight is being reflected into the living space through the windows.

  This happens in a subtle, yet uniform manner, which creates a pleasant atmosphere.
- Minimal artificial light is used, only around the sitting area.
- Specs: 8 m x 13 m x 3 m

A3 and A5

- As a weekend getaway, the design of the space is intended to remain closed during the week, and in the weekend, opens up through manually operated shades.

A4

- The courtyard has manually operated canvas which helps in partial shading and allows for outdoor seating during the day.

A8

- Narrow horizontal windows are facing the South to reduce heat gain.

Challenges:

- Glare because of poor protection from the upper end of the floor-to-ceiling windows.
- Although shading mechanisms are used in the East-West windows, heat transfer is still a strong factor to be considered.

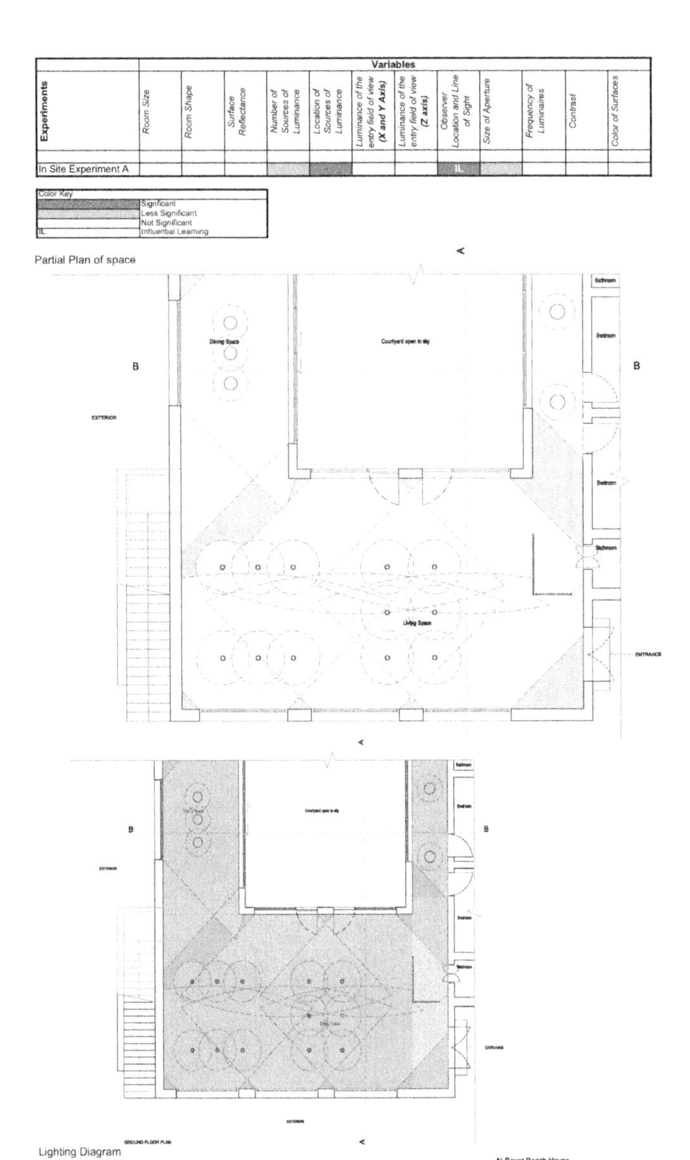

Experiments	Variables											
	Room Size	Room Shape	Surface Reflectance	Number of Sources of Luminance	Location of Sources of Luminance	Luminance of the entry field of view **(X and Y Axis)**	Luminance of the entry field of view **(Z axis)**	Observer Location and Line of Sight	Size of Aperture	Frequency of Luminaires	Contrast	Color of Surfaces
In Site Experiment A								IL				

Color Key	
	Signficant
	Less Significant
	Not Significant
IL	Influential Learning

Partial Plan of space

Lighting Diagram

Al-Sayer Beach House

Experiments	Variables											
	Room Size	*Room Shape*	*Surface Reflectance*	*Number of Sources of Luminance*	*Location of Sources of Luminance*	*Luminance of the entry field of view* ***(X and Y Axis)***	*Luminance of the entry field of view* ***(Z axis)***	*Observer Location and Line of Sight*	*Size of Aperture*	*Frequency of Luminaires*	*Contrast*	*Color of Surfaces*
In Site Experiment A								IL				

Color Key	
	Significant
	Less Significant
	Not Significant
IL	Influential Learning

A1

A2

Experiments	Variables											
	Room Size	Room Shape	Surface Reflectance	Number of Sources of Luminance	Location of Sources of Luminance	Luminance of the entry field of view **(X and Y Axis)**	Luminance of the entry field of view **(Z axis)**	Observer Location and Line of Sight	Size of Aperture	Frequency of Luminaires	Contrast	Color of Surfaces
In Site Experiment A								IL				

Color Key	
	Significant
	Less Significant
	Not Significant
IL	Influential Learning

A7

A6

	Variables											
Experiments	*Room Size*	*Room Shape*	*Surface Reflectance*	*Number of Sources of Luminance*	*Location of Sources of Luminance*	*Luminance of the entry field of view* ***(X and Y Axis)***	*Luminance of the entry field of view* ***(Z axis)***	*Observer Location and Line of Sight*	*Size of Aperture*	*Frequency of Luminaires*	*Contrast*	*Color of Surfaces*
In Site Experiment A								IL				

Color Key	
	Significant
	Less Significant
	Not Significant
IL	Influential Learning

A4

A8

INSITE EXPERIMENT C – INSTANT OFFICES

General Overview / Objective:

- Speculative office space designed on a module basis of 3m x 4m offices to be leased to various tenants.
- Divided into four clusters - Each cluster is oriented towards a different view / orientation (North / South / East / West)
- The four clusters revolve around a central atrium which overlooks the lower levels of the mall.

  The atrium is covered by a glazed roof which allows through plenty of heat and light.
- Categorized as medium budget office space.
- Location in Dar Al Awadhi, Kuwait City
- Specs: 1800 m2 situated on the 4th floor of a retail center

In order to best tackle the very bright Atrium, the corridors and the lobby were designed as a threshold to allow for greater adaptation space for the eyes before reaching the office cells.

Question: How to design speculative office cells with various tenants in an enclosure of a very bright atrium?

Applicable Variables:

- Surface Reflectance
- Number of Sources of Luminance
- **Location of Sources of Luminance (IL)**

- **Observer Location and Line of Sight (IL)**
- **Frequency of Luminaires (IL)**
- **Contrast (IL)**
- **Color of Surfaces (IL)**

Influential Learning:

By manipulating the threshold between the very bright daylit (through a sky light) / artificially lit atrium and the individual office space through the use of contrasting colors and brightness, the transition between both spaces were designed to enhance the visual comfort.

In that threshold, artificial light was added at the entrance of each office to:

- Introduce the opening of a new space
- Create an artificial light rhythm in the corridor

C1, C2 and C3

- The Atrium allows a lot of natural through from the roof.
- The circulation space around the Atrium is perceived as very dark by users due to the contrast between the Atrium and the circulation space.
- This created a need to add many artificial lights

C4

- To respond to the bright Atrium, within the four clusters a series of offices are designed which are accessed through double loaded corridor. The corridors connect the two lobbies / entrances of each cluster.

Refer to separate light readings on each cluster

C5 and C6

- Exhibit of how bright the Atrium is from the perspective of someone in the office.

C7, C8, C9 and C14

- Creating and 'stretching' the threshold space between the office space and the Atrium. Design technique included:
- Non-reflective grey painted walls / ceilings / doors
- Lighter grey carpet flooring
- Accustomed light fittings has been designed and manufactured to be placed on top of each of the doors to highlight the entrance and create a continuous alteration between light and dark sequence.

C10

- By entering office space from the grey-painted corridor, the office is automatically perceived as being brighter.
- This is due to light adaptation. Creating the notion of moving from a dark space (corridor) to a lighter one (the office) helps to mitigate the extra bright Atrium.
- This helps achieve the comfort level necessary for the office space.

C11, C12 and C13

- Non-reflective white painted walls / ceilings
- Light grey carpet flooring

- The office cell is designed to suit a minimum of 1 employee / maximum of 3 employees within the exhibited work stations.
- The surface area on the work station is a very light white grey laminate.
- The office has manually operated 5% light imitance roller shades which is individually operated.
- The lights within the offices are down lights which are placed on top of the working space in addition to the task lights for individual use.

Challenges:

- Atrium allows through plenty of heat and light.
- Since the offices were retro-fitted in an existing building, minimal if not nonexistent ability to redesign the shell of the space.
- This lack of flexibility caused certain offices to remain 'unused' due to intense brightness.
- In addition, due to the restrictions from the client, offices were not supposed to be designed differently, they had to be all uniform, posing further limitation to respond to the particular challenges of each cell.

Experiments	Variables											
	Room Size	Room Shape	Surface Reflectance	Number of Sources of Luminance	Location of Sources of Luminance	Luminance of the entry field of view **(X and Y Axis)**	Luminance of the entry field of view **(Z axis)**	Observer Location and Line of Sight	Size of Aperture	Frequency of Luminaires	Contrast	Color of Surfaces
In Site Experiment C					IL			IL		IL	IL	IL

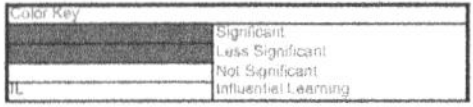
Color Key

	Significant
	Less Significant
	Not Significant
IL	Influential Learning

C2 C3

C1

Experiments	Variables											
	Room Size	Room Shape	Surface Reflectance	Number of Sources of Luminance	Location of Sources of Luminance	Luminance of the entry field of view **(X and Y Axis)**	Luminance of the entry field of view **(Z axis)**	Observer Location and Line of Sight	Size of Aperture	Frequency of Luminaires	Contrast	Color of Surfaces
In Site Experiment C					IL			IL		IL	IL	IL

Color Key	
	Significant
	Less Significant
	Not Significant
IL	Influential Learning

c4

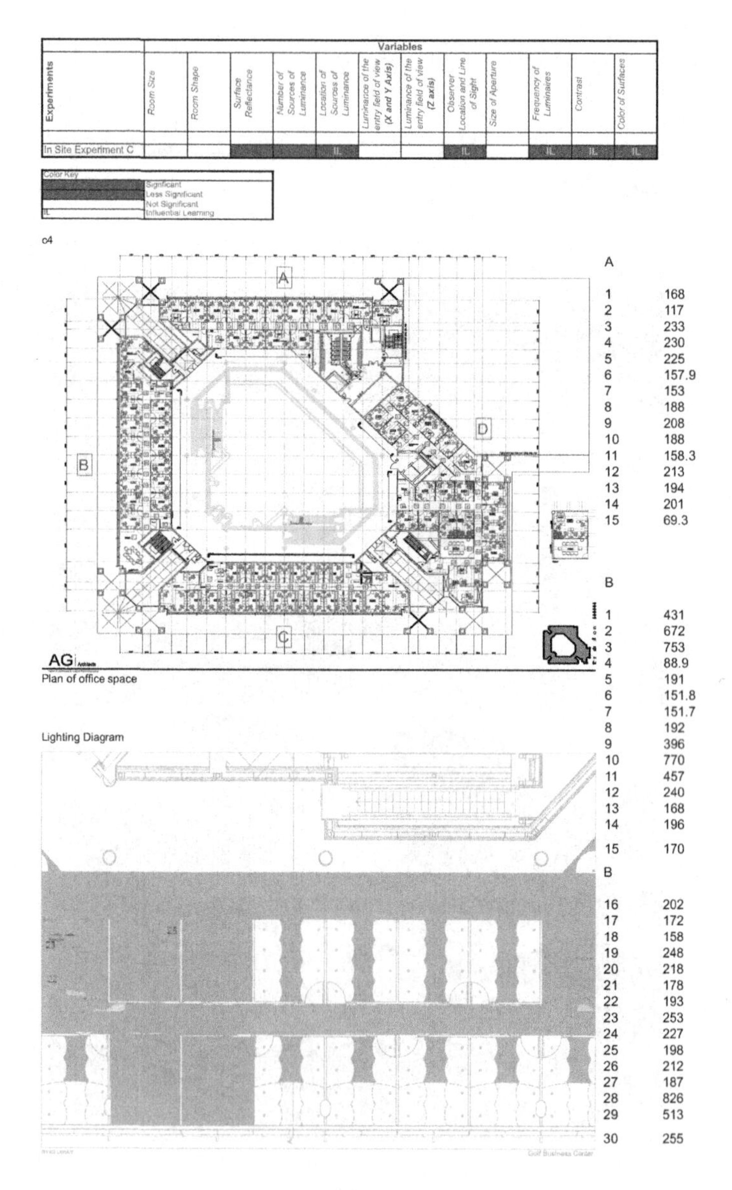

Plan of office space

Lighting Diagram

A	
1	168
2	117
3	233
4	230
5	225
6	157.9
7	153
8	188
9	208
10	188
11	158.3
12	213
13	194
14	201
15	69.3

B	
1	431
2	672
3	753
4	88.9
5	191
6	151.8
7	151.7
8	192
9	396
10	770
11	457
12	240
13	168
14	196
15	170

B	
16	202
17	172
18	158
19	248
20	218
21	178
22	193
23	253
24	227
25	198
26	212
27	187
28	826
29	513
30	255

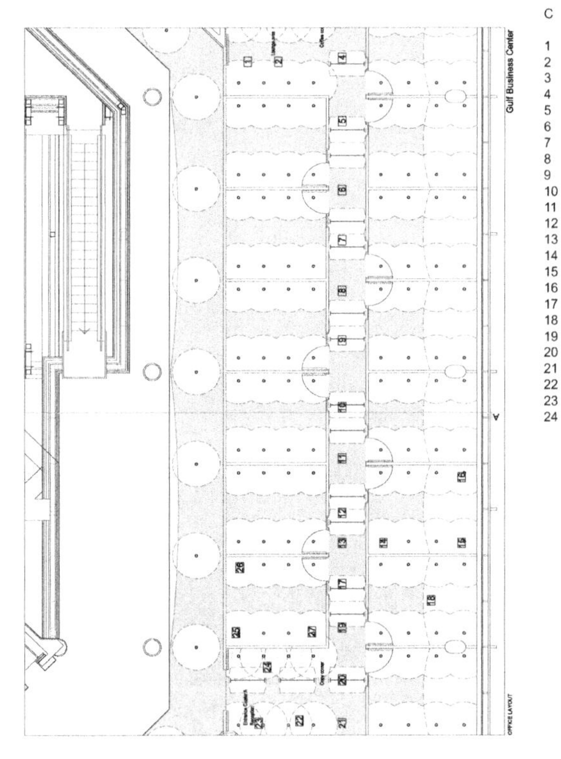

	C
1	225
2	208
3	203
4	124.8
5	181
6	143.1
7	167.7
8	137
9	164
10	163.4
11	147
12	176
13	165.3
14	280
15	660
16	498
17	173.4
18	402
19	163.5
20	185
21	105
22	112
23	104
24	151.2

Partial Plan of office space, Lighting Study

Section: Lighting Study

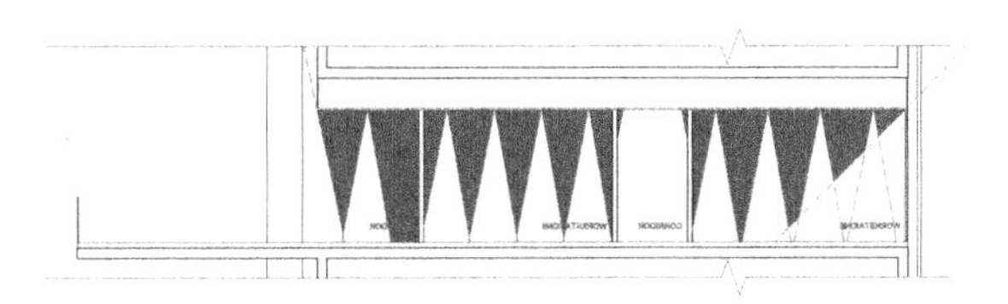

	Variables											
Experiments	*Room Size*	*Room Shape*	*Surface Reflectance*	*Number of Sources of Luminance*	*Location of Sources of Luminance*	*Luminance of the entry field of view* ***(X and Y Axis)***	*Luminance of the entry field of view* ***(Z axis)***	*Observer Location and Line of Sight*	*Size of Aperture*	*Frequency of Luminaires*	*Contrast*	*Color of Surfaces*
In Site Experiment C					IL			IL		IL	IL	IL

Color Key	
	Significant
	Less Significant
	Not Significant
IL	Influential Learning

C5

C6

	Variables											
Experiments	Room Size	Room Shape	Surface Reflectance	Number of Sources of Luminance	Location of Sources of Luminance	Luminance of the entry field of view **(X and Y Axis)**	Luminance of the entry field of view **(Z axis)**	Observer Location and Line of Sight	Size of Aperture	Frequency of Luminaires	Contrast	Color of Surfaces
In Site Experiment C					IL			IL		IL	IL	IL

Color Key	
	Significant
	Less Significant
	Not Significant
IL	Influential Learning

C7

C8

C9

C14

Experiments	Variables											
	Room Size	Room Shape	Surface Reflectance	Number of Sources of Luminance	Location of Sources of Luminance	Luminance of the entry field of view **(X and Y Axis)**	Luminance of the entry field of view **(Z axis)**	Observer Location and Line of Sight	Size of Aperture	Frequency of Luminaires	Contrast	Color of Surfaces
In Site Experiment C					IL			IL		IL	IL	IL

Color Key	
	Significant
	Less Significant
	Not Significant
IL	Influential Learning

C10 C11

D	
1	219
2	183
3	150
4	174
5	280
6	165
7	185
8	137
9	121.8
10	222
11	89
12	114.2
13	169
14	81
15	153
16	165
17	126
18	178
19	172.5
20	84.4
21	176.7
22	271
23	225
24	229
25	328
D	
26	212
27	140
28	124.3
29	168
30	330
31	460
32	270
33	218
34	218
35	457
36	864
37	987
38	310
39	128.3
40	101.7
41	150.7
42	95
43	270
44	333
45	279
46	314
47	297
48	550
49	141.9
50	496

Experiments	Variables												
	Room Size	Room Shape	Surface Reflectance	Number of Sources of Luminance	Location of Sources of Luminance	Luminance of the entry field of view **(X and Y Axis)**	Luminance of the entry field of view **(Z axis)**	Observer Location and Line of Sight	Size of Aperture	Frequency of Luminaires	Contrast	Color of Surfaces
In Site Experiment C					IL			IL		IL	IL	IL

Color Key	
	Significant
	Less Significant
	Not Significant
IL	Influential Learning

C12

C12 xxxx

INSITE EXPERIMENT D – LA OFICINA

General Overview / Objectives:

- Renovation of an existing warehouse in an industrial area into a speculative office building with multiple tenants.
- Building experienced an overhaul of its interior space.
- Introduction of horizontal windows in the façade and cladding the exterior façade with sandstone.
- Categorized as low budget office space.
- Location: Al Rai, Kuwait
- Specs: 2000 m2 office building

Question: How do we move from an exgterior of more than 10,000 lux to an office space with an average 300 lux?

Applicable Variables:

- Surface Reflectance
- **Number of Sources of Luminance (IL)**
- Location of Sources of Luminance
- **Luminance of the Entry Field View Z Axis (IL)**
- **Observer location of Line of Sight (IL)**
- **Contrast (IL)**
- **Color of Surfaces (IL)**

Influential Learning:

In order to mitigate the extreme light levels between the exterior and the interior, a sudden decrease due to contrast ratios and a very dark lobby to a gradual lighter phased out environment. (ie. Stairway / corridor etc.)

D1, D2, D8 and D14

- Exhibits the main entrance from the main street
- A metal canopy is introduced to shade the main entrance.
- Shading devices were introduced to protect all the main windows depending on their orientation. These devices were horizontal metal sheets, similar to the canopy.

D3 and D4

- The main lobby is designed for a 'short-term' transit point before heading off to the various offices.
- Very minimal seating space is made available.
- Darker space is created – natural light is introduced into the space through only one opening – (the main door).
- The flooring is made up of dark non reflective grey ceramic tiles, and white walls and ceilings.
- Very little artificial light is used to compensate
- Only 2 task lights are placed for the receptionist seated in the lobby.
- Initial reaction for a user is to experience a sudden level of darkness – this is intended to 'interrupt' the bright exterior.

D5 and D6

- The stair wall is painted with black non-reflective walls and black non-reflective stone walls.
- The stair landings have one wall which is painted white and have minimum light to direct focus to the wall itself.
- Within this space, the brightness is interrupted.

D7 and D9

- From the stairs, you look into the corridor, and see two sequences. That of the corridor and the sequence of the space behind it
- The corridor slowly begins to introduce additional light to prepare the user for the entrance of the offices.
- The cove lights are placed parallel to the corridor
- *From the corridor various office types could be reached.*

D10 – AGI Offices

- Office orientation is South
- 50 m2 office space with 5m x 2m window overlooking the back alley
- Electronically operated roller shades
- The office consists of work stations with VDTs which are lit by task lights
- Central meeting / exhibit table using track lights
- Space is perceived brightly. Use of artificial light is minimal, used in the late afternoon.

D11 and D12 – MS Holding

- 24 m2 Office orientation is North.
- Fully glazed windows 8m x 2.40m and 4m x 2.40m / electronically operated roller shades.
- Wooden laminated floor with white walls and ceiling.
- Comfortable bright room, despite roller blinds, that requires virtually **no** artificial light (due to northern orientation and size of window)

D13 and *D14* – MS Retail

- Typical office cell on ground floor.
- Office orientation is South.
- High horizontal window which is located at the top of the ceiling. This is intentionally designed to reflect off of the light rays on the metal shading (see D2) of the window. This acts like a light shelf.
- This brings in more reflected light into the space, creating a slightly softer ambience than direct sun light.

Challenges:

- Lack of control in building design, since it was a renovated warehouse
- Difficulty in managing limited individual control
- Managed however to control the size of the window depending on the orientation, as well as the sun shading mechanisms.

Experiments	Variables											
	Room Size	Room Shape	Surface Reflectance	Number of Sources of Luminance	Location of Sources of Luminance	Luminance of the entry field of view **(X and Y Axis)**	Luminance of the entry field of view **(Z axis)**	Observer Location and Line of Sight	Size of Aperture	Frequency of Luminaires	Contrast	Color of Surfaces
In Site Experiment D					IL			IL			IL	IL

Color Key	
	Significant
	Less Significant
	Not Significant
IL	Influential Learning

D1

D14

Experiments	Variables											
	Room Size	Room Shape	Surface Reflectance	Number of Sources of Luminance	Location of Sources of Luminance	Luminance of the entry field of view **(X and Y Axis)**	Luminance of the entry field of view **(Z axis)**	Observer Location and Line of Sight	Size of Aperture	Frequency of Luminaires	Contrast	Color of Surfaces
In Site Experiment D					IL			IL			IL	IL

Color Key	
	Significant
	Less Significant
	Not Significant
IL	Influential Learning

C2

C8

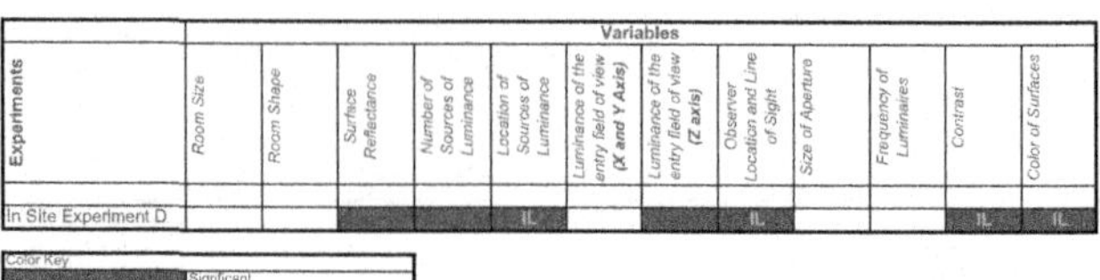

Experiments	Variables											
	Room Size	Room Shape	Surface Reflectance	Number of Sources of Luminance	Location of Sources of Luminance	Luminance of the entry field of view **(X and Y Axis)**	Luminance of the entry field of view **(Z axis)**	Observer Location and Line of Sight	Size of Aperture	Frequency of Luminaires	Contrast	Color of Surfaces
In Site Experiment D					IL			IL			IL	IL

Color Key	
	Significant
	Less Significant
	Not Significant
IL	Influential Learning

Lighting Diagram

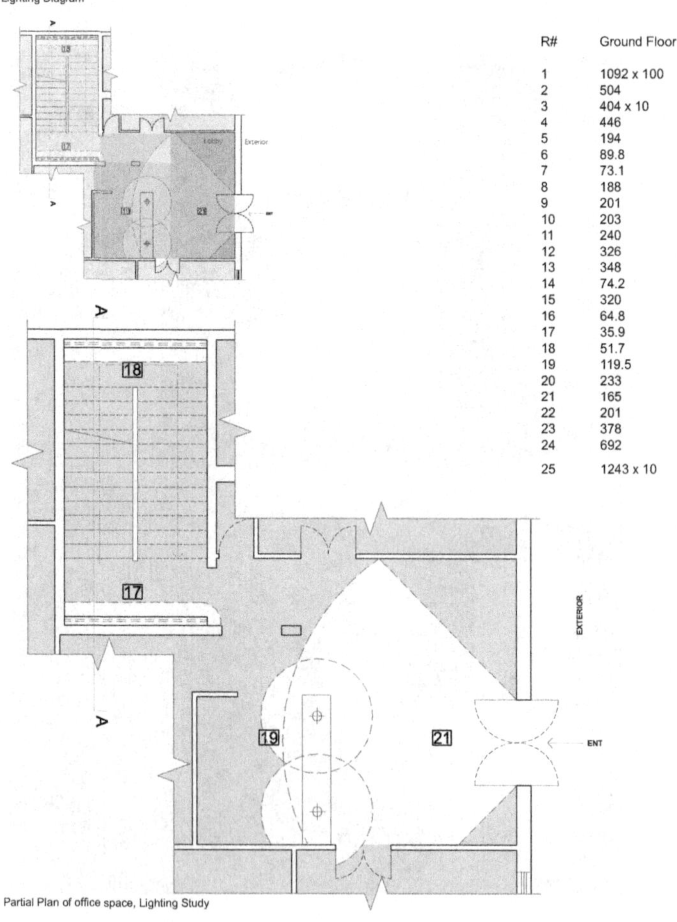

R#	Ground Floor
1	1092 x 100
2	504
3	404 x 10
4	446
5	194
6	89.8
7	73.1
8	188
9	201
10	203
11	240
12	326
13	348
14	74.2
15	320
16	64.8
17	35.9
18	51.7
19	119.5
20	233
21	165
22	201
23	378
24	692
25	1243 x 10

Partial Plan of office space, Lighting Study

Experiments	Variables											
	Room Size	Room Shape	Surface Reflectance	Number of Sources of Luminance	Location of Sources of Luminance	Luminance of the entry field of view **(X and Y Axis)**	Luminance of the entry field of view **(Z axis)**	Observer Location and Line of Sight	Size of Aperture	Frequency of Luminaires	Contrast	Color of Surfaces
In Site Experiment D					IL			IL			IL	IL

Color Key	
	Significant
	Less Significant
	Not Significant
IL	Influential Learning

D3

D4

Experiments	Variables											
	Room Size	*Room Shape*	*Surface Reflectance*	*Number of Sources of Luminance*	*Location of Sources of Luminance*	*Luminance of the entry field of view* **(X and Y Axis)**	*Luminance of the entry field of view* **(Z axis)**	*Observer Location and Line of Sight*	*Size of Aperture*	*Frequency of Luminaires*	*Contrast*	*Color of Surfaces*
In Site Experiment D					IL			IL			IL	IL

Color Key	
	Significant
	Less Significant
	Not Significant
IL	Influential Learning

Section, Lighting Diagram

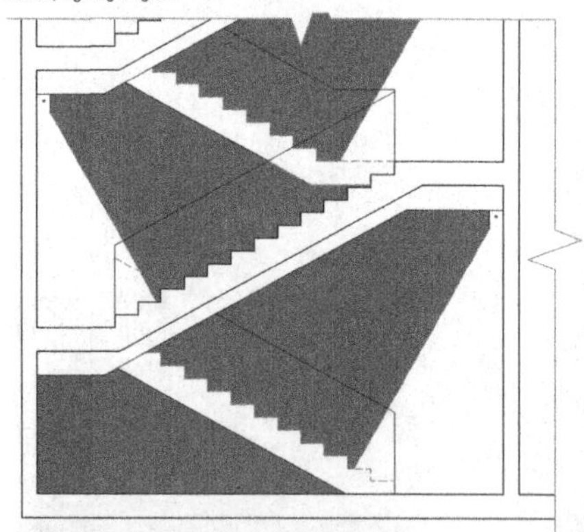

D5 D6

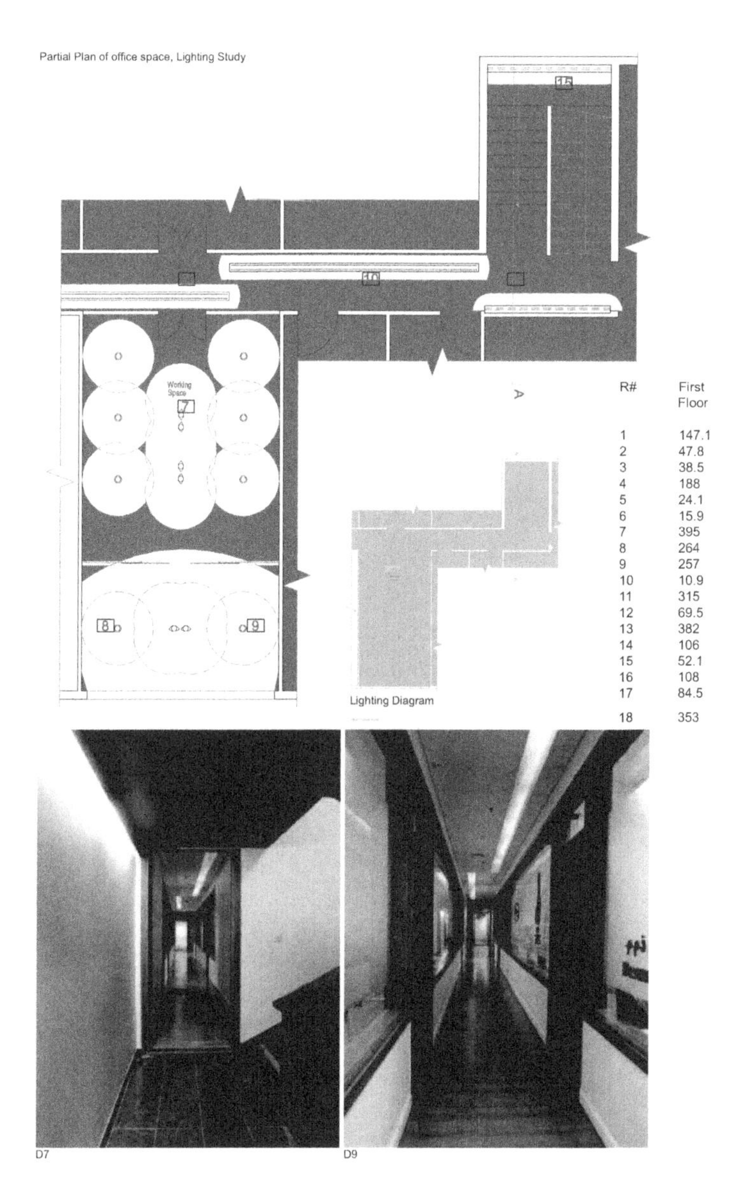

R#	First Floor
1	147.1
2	47.8
3	38.5
4	188
5	24.1
6	15.9
7	395
8	264
9	257
10	10.9
11	315
12	69.5
13	382
14	106
15	52.1
16	108
17	84.5
18	353

D7

D9

Experiments	Variables											
	Room Size	Room Shape	Surface Reflectance	Number of Sources of Luminance	Location of Sources of Luminance	Luminance of the entry field of view **(X and Y Axis)**	Luminance of the entry field of view **(Z axis)**	Observer Location and Line of Sight	Size of Aperture	Frequency of Luminaires	Contrast	Color of Surfaces
In Site Experiment D					IL			IL			IL	IL

Color Key	
	Significant
	Less Significant
	Not Significant
IL	Influential Learning

Experiments	Variables											
	Room Size	Room Shape	Surface Reflectance	Number of Sources of Luminance	Location of Sources of Luminance	Luminance of the entry field of view **(X and Y Axis)**	Luminance of the entry field of view **(Z axis)**	Observer Location and Line of Sight	Size of Aperture	Frequency of Luminaires	Contrast	Color of Surfaces
In Site Experiment D					IL			IL			IL	IL

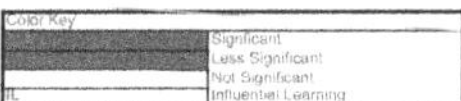

Color Key	
	Significant
	Less Significant
	Not Significant
IL	Influential Learning

C13

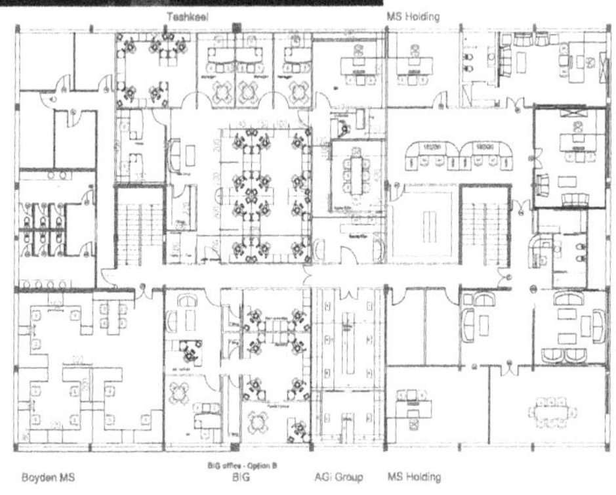

C15

INSITE EXPERIMENT E – AL GHANIM INDUSTRIES – KUWAIT FREE TRADE ZONE

General Overview / Objective:
E1, E2, E3, E4 and E5

- 1500 m2 office space with orientation of the North / East / West
- AGI work included interior renovation of an existing building.
- The users are engineers who require work stations to operate their computers and review their drawings.
- Internally, manually operated 5% light imitance roller shades for floor to ceiling windows **(throughout the whole façade with a height of 4m)** were introduced.
- Non-reflective white walls and ceilings and dark beige carpet floorings were used
- Lights were suspended to heights of 2.40m to illuminate the work stations directly to create comfortable light levels
- Additional lights were introduced along the passages

Question: How do we adapt an existing office space with full glazed windows into a comfortable work place?

Applicable Variables;

- Surface Reflectance
- Number of Sources of Luminance
- Location of Sources of Luminance
- Luminance of the Entry Field of View Z Axis
- Size of Aperture
- Frequency of Luminaires

Influential Learning: None of the variables are considered influential learnings due to the limitations that the pre-existed space imposed on the design.

Challenges:

- Convert a 'glass box' with tinted green glass into a comfortable office environment.
- This environment creates a very bright luminosity levels in the work stations even though it is perceived by the human eye as very dark.
- This necessitated the use of more artificial light.
- In addition, since the floor plate is very deep, the natural light did not travel evenly throughout the space, which caused the dependence on artificial light within the space.

Insight

- This exhibit highlights the inadequacies of a direct 'copy-paste' approach to design using western conventional lighting techniques, (ie floor to ceiling windows)
- This exhibit also accentuates the light adaptation, further showing the natural reaction of human visual physiology.

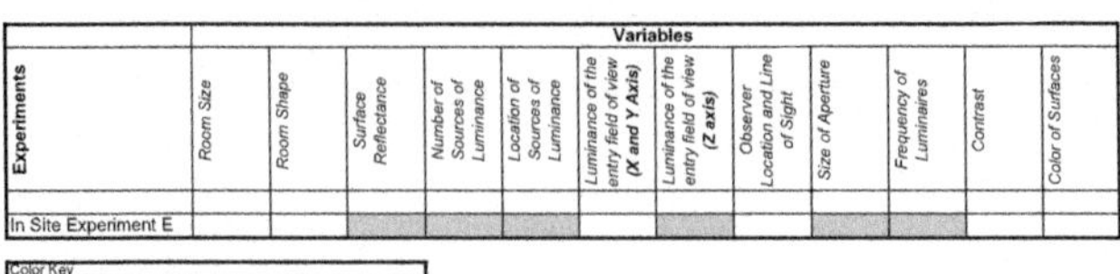

Experiments	Variables											
	Room Size	Room Shape	Surface Reflectance	Number of Sources of Luminance	Location of Sources of Luminance	Luminance of the entry field of view **(X and Y Axis)**	Luminance of the entry field of view **(Z axis)**	Observer Location and Line of Sight	Size of Aperture	Frequency of Luminaires	Contrast	Color of Surfaces
In Site Experiment E												

Color Key	
	Significant
	Less Significant
	Not Significant
IL	Influential Learning

Partial Plan of office space, Lighting Study

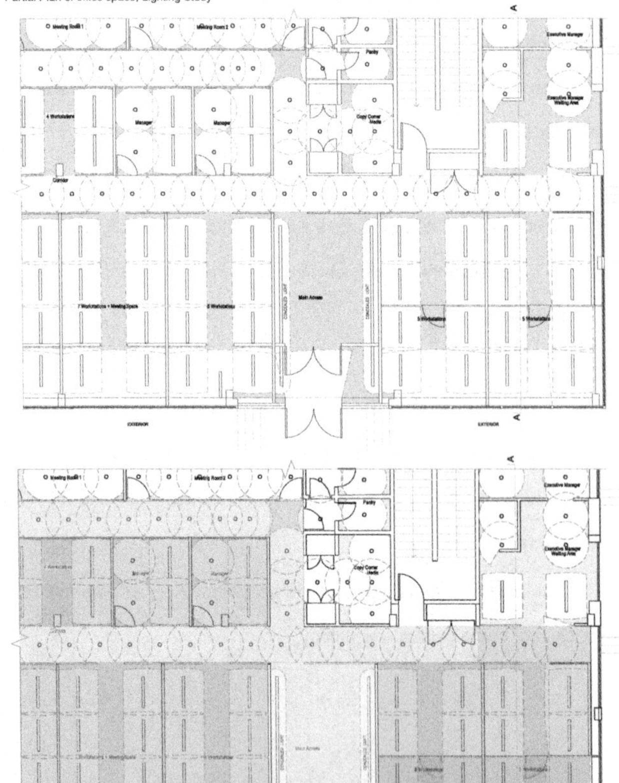

Lighting Diagram

Section

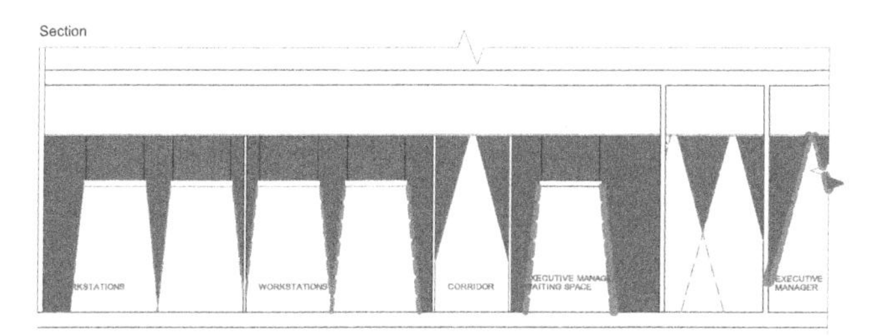

E1

E2

Experiments	Variables											
	Room Size	Room Shape	Surface Reflectance	Number of Sources of Luminance	Location of Sources of Luminance	Luminance of the entry field of view **(X and Y Axis)**	Luminance of the entry field of view **(Z axis)**	Observer Location and Line of Sight	Size of Aperture	Frequency of Luminaires	Contrast	Color of Surfaces
In Site Experiment E												

Color Key	
	Significant
	Less Significant
	Not Significant
IL	Influential Learning

E4

E5

E6

INSITE EXPERIMENT F – BEDROOM EXTENSION

General Overview / Objective:

- A 50 m2 room studio extension to an existing 1980's house in the suburbs Bayan, Kuwait.
- The studio consists of living, sleeping and working spaces.
- Surrounded by service areas of the neighbors' houses except for the Eastern orientation where one window is placed.
- The size of the window is 3m x 3m

Question: How to deliver daylight to various task locations within a bedroom?

Applicable Variables:

- Room Size
- Room Shape
- Surface Reflectance
- Number of Source of Luminance
- Location of Source of Luminance
- Luminance of the Entry Field of x and y axis
- Luminance of the Entry Field of z axis
- Observer Location and Line of Sight
- **Size of Aperture (IL)**
- Frequency of Luminaires
- **Contrast (IL)**
- Color of Surfaces

Influential Learning: To increase visual comfort, it is important to locate various daylight sources, aperture sizes complemented by differentiating contrast and color

F1

- Intentionally dark entrance
- Used dark wooden floors and doors

F2, F3 and F4

- The room consists of a sitting and sleeping area.
- One window overlooks the garden
- Due to the depth of the space, two skylights were introduced and one small side light window to bring daylight.
- The first skylight is designed to capture Northern light into the back of the sitting area.
- The second skylight is designed to capture Eastern and Western sunlight into the changing / power room area (these are the times it is primarily used)

F11

- Artificial light (task light) is available on top the study area, as well as the powder room and the bathroom.
- 4 spot lights are distributed on top of the coffee table and the changing room.
- Bed side tables also have task lights.

F5, F6, F7, F8, F9 and F10

- The main window overlooking the garden has manually operated roller blinds to control the Eastern sunlight coming into the room.

Insight

- Due to the multiple light sources which bring in light from various angles, the room is very comfortably luminated throughout the day.
- This punctual distribution of the light sources in an uneven manner is comfortable to the eye as the different sources complement one another.
- The room experiences drastic levels of brightness which is controlled through the roller blinds of the available window. This provides a comfortable, simple, and very pleasant ambience.

Experiments	Variables												
	Room Size	*Room Shape*	*Surface Reflectance*	*Number of Sources of Luminance*	*Location of Sources of Luminance*	*Luminance of the entry field of view* ***(X and Y Axis)***	*Luminance of the entry field of view* ***(Z axis)***	*Observer Location and Line of Sight*	*Size of Aperture*	*Frequency of Luminaires*	*Contrast*	*Color of Surfaces*
In Site Experiment F									IL		IL	

Color Key	
	Signficant
	Less Significant
	Not Significant
IL	Influential Learning

F1

F2

Plan of Space, Lighting Study

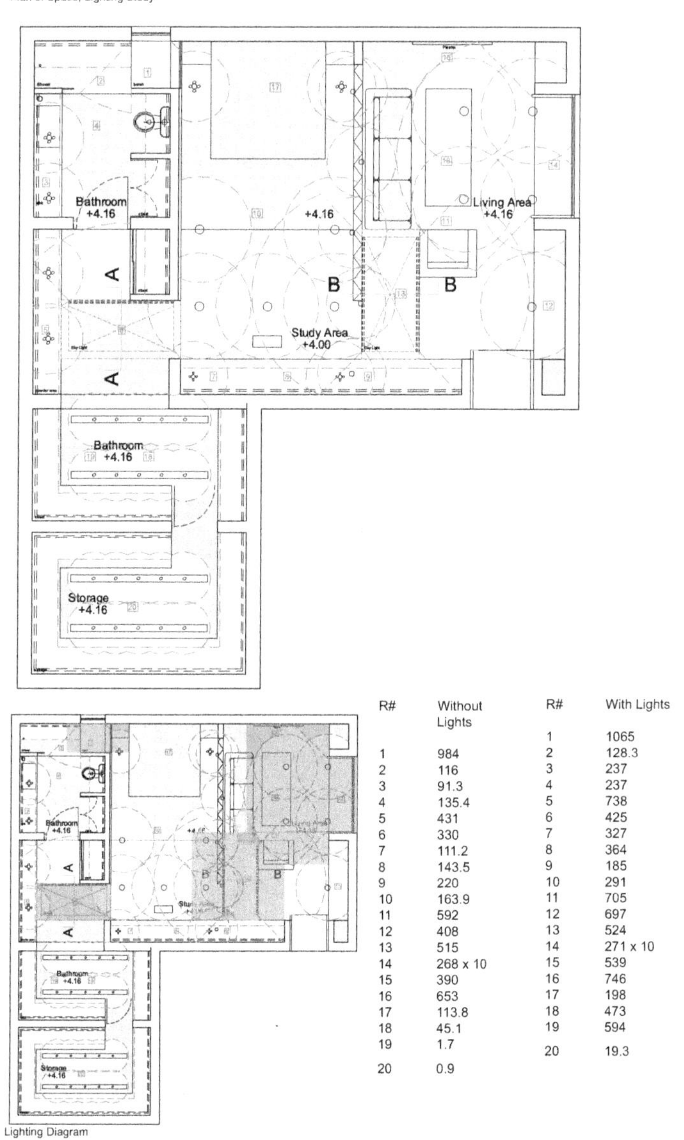

Lighting Diagram

R#	Without Lights	R#	With Lights
1	984	1	1065
2	116	2	128.3
3	91.3	3	237
4	135.4	4	237
5	431	5	738
6	330	6	425
7	111.2	7	327
8	143.5	8	364
9	220	9	185
10	163.9	10	291
11	592	11	705
12	408	12	697
13	515	13	524
14	268 x 10	14	271 x 10
15	390	15	539
16	653	16	746
17	113.8	17	198
18	45.1	18	473
19	1.7	19	594
20	0.9	20	19.3

Sections thourgh the two Sky Lights

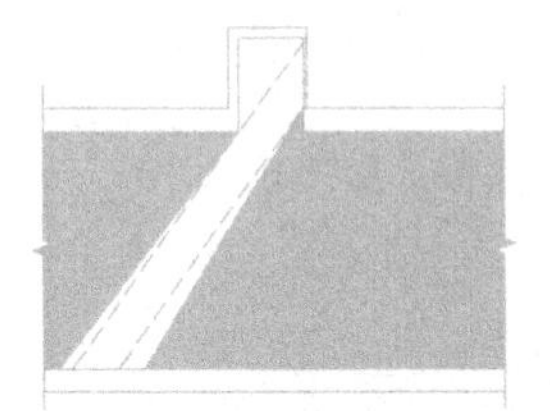

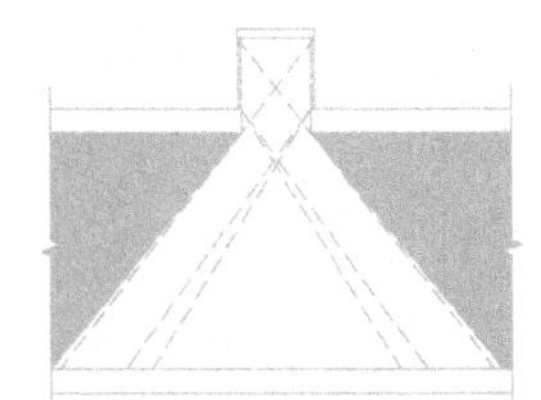

F3

F4

Experiments	Variables											
	Room Size	Room Shape	Surface Reflectance	Number of Sources of Luminance	Location of Sources of Luminance	Luminance of the entry field of view **(X and Y Axis)**	Luminance of the entry field of view **(Z axis)**	Observer Location and Line of Sight	Size of Aperture	Frequency of Luminaires	Contrast	Color of Surfaces
In Site Experiment F									IL		IL	

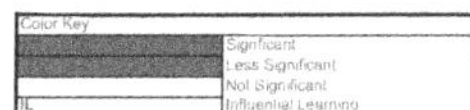

Color Key	
	Signficant
	Less Significant
	Not Significant
IL	Influential Learning

F11

F12

Experiments	Variables											
	Room Size	Room Shape	Surface Reflectance	Number of Sources of Luminance	Location of Sources of Luminance	Luminance of the entry field of view **(X and Y Axis)**	Luminance of the entry field of view **(Z axis)**	Observer Location and Line of Sight	Size of Aperture	Frequency of Luminaires	Contrast	Color of Surfaces
In Site Experiment F									IL		IL	

Color Key	
	Signficant
	Less Significant
	Not Significant
IL	Influential Learning

F6

F7

F8

F9

INSITE EXPERIMENT G – AL RAI ONE

General Overview / Objective:

- The building is a speculative office building.
- Basement, ground and first floor.
- 1200 m2 located in Al Rai, Kuwait.

Question: How to design an office space which allows comfortable daylight without increasing heat gain and disturbing visual comfort?

Applicable Variables:

- Room Size
- Room Shape
- Surface Reflectance
- Number of Source of Luminance
- Location of Source of Luminance
- Luminance of the Entry Field of x and y axis
- Luminance of the Entry Field of z axis
- Size of Aperture
- Contrast
- Color of Surfaces

Influential Learning: *Building Currently Under Construction.* The 10 meter depth of the floor plate is providing enough light distribution for the entire space. The findings will be tested as soon as the building is complete.

G1

- Building under construction – facing all orientations (North, South, East and West)

- For the most optimum use of the light in the office space, the façade was punctured with 60cm high and various length windows at desk and ceiling level. (learning lesson from Exhibit F)
- The strip windows mitigate the heat transfer due to the narrowness of the window, hence positioning itself always in shadow.
- Various heights of windows assure that the light is directly focused on a seated person or on illuminating the ceiling plane.
- Due to the narrow width of the office plate, light will distribute along the depth of the building.

G2

- Light is introduced in the (elevated 1.50m from ground) basement through horizontal strip windows which run along the façade of the building.

G3

- A sunken courtyard designed to bring indirect natural light into the work space.

G4

- Skylight introduced to add additional light source because of the depth of the space.

G5

- Light is introduced in the first floor through horizontal strip windows that run along the façade of the building.
- The light sources are placed on two different levels – one on the desk level (90cm) and at finished ceiling level (200 cm).

G6

- A courtyard in the roof attracts reflected light into the back part of the office space.

- Similar to the ground floor, light sources are placed on two separate levels.

Challenges:

- Drawback of G3: Space is very deep and the light source is only at one edge. Compensation necessary with multiple artificial light.
- This problem was mitigated in the floor above by introducing a skylight (G4)

Experiments	Variables											
	Room Size	*Room Shape*	*Surface Reflectance*	*Number of Sources of Luminance*	*Location of Sources of Luminance*	*Luminance of the entry field of view* ***(X and Y Axis)***	*Luminance of the entry field of view* ***(Z axis)***	*Observer Location and Line of Sight*	*Size of Aperture*	*Frequency of Luminaires*	*Contrast*	*Color of Surfaces*
In Site Experiment G												

Color Key	
	Significant
	Less Significant
	Not Significant
IL	Influential Learning

G1

G1

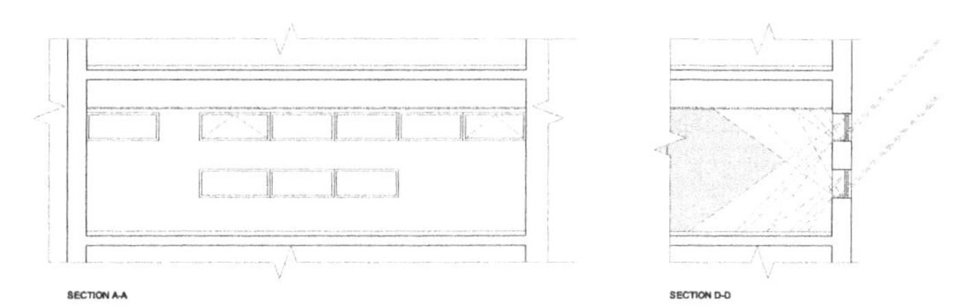

Elevation and Section of Typical office

Partial Plan of office space, Lighting Study

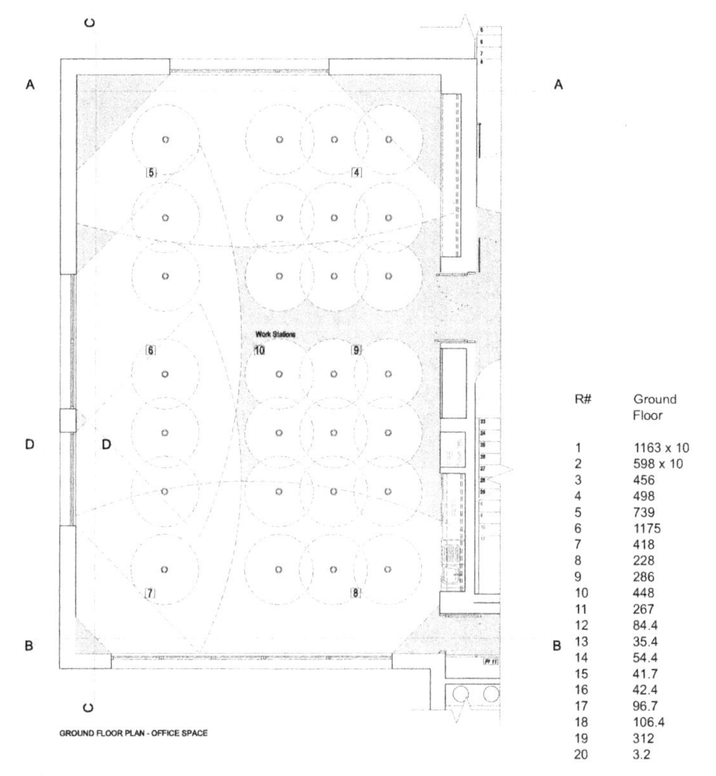

R#	Ground Floor
1	1163 x 10
2	598 x 10
3	456
4	498
5	739
6	1175
7	418
8	228
9	286
10	448
11	267
12	84.4
13	35.4
14	54.4
15	41.7
16	42.4
17	96.7
18	106.4
19	312
20	3.2

Experiments	Variables											
	Room Size	Room Shape	Surface Reflectance	Number of Sources of Luminance	Location of Sources of Luminance	Luminance of the entry field of view **(X and Y Axis)**	Luminance of the entry field of view **(Z axis)**	Observer Location and Line of Sight	Size of Aperture	Frequency of Luminaires	Contrast	Color of Surfaces
In Site Experiment G												

Color Key	
	Significant
	Less Significant
	Not Significant
IL	Influential Learning

G2

G2

R#	Basement
1	418 x 10
2	676
3	400
4	734
5	486
6	403
7	298
8	133
9	56.2
10	34.2
11	9.8
12	6.6
13	7.2
14	4.8
15	4.5
16	68.4
17	79
18	12.3
19	370
20	767
21	526
22	234
23	487
24	328
25	491

Experiments	Variables											
	Room Size	Room Shape	Surface Reflectance	Number of Sources of Luminance	Location of Sources of Luminance	Luminance of the entry field of view **(X and Y Axis)**	Luminance of the entry field of view **(Z axis)**	Observer Location and Line of Sight	Size of Aperture	Frequency of Luminaires	Contrast	Color of Surfaces
In Site Expenment G												

Color Key	
	Significant
	Less Significant
	Not Significant
IL	Influential Learning

Light Diagrams

G3

Experiments	Variables											
	Room Size	Room Shape	Surface Reflectance	Number of Sources of Luminance	Location of Sources of Luminance	Luminance of the entry field of view **(X and Y Axis)**	Luminance of the entry field of view **(Z axis)**	Observer Location and Line of Sight	Size of Aperture	Frequency of Luminaires	Contrast	Color of Surfaces
In Site Experiment G												

Color Key	
	Significant
	Less Significant
	Not Significant
IL	Influential Learning

G5

G5 G5

Experiments	Variables											
	Room Size	Room Shape	Surface Reflectance	Number of Sources of Luminance	Location of Sources of Luminance	Luminance of the entry field of view **(X and Y Axis)**	Luminance of the entry field of view **(Z axis)**	Observer Location and Line of Sight	Size of Aperture	Frequency of Luminaires	Contrast	Color of Surfaces
In Site Experiment G												

Color Key	
	Significant
	Less Significant
	Not Significant
IL	Influential Learning

G5

G5

Experiments	Variables												
	Room Size	Room Shape	Surface Reflectance	Number of Sources of Luminance	Location of Sources of Luminance	Luminance of the entry field of view **(X and Y Axis)**	Luminance of the entry field of view **(Z axis)**	Observer Location and Line of Sight	Size of Aperture	Frequency of Luminaires	Contrast	Color of Surfaces
In Site Experiment G												

Color Key	
	Significant
	Less Significant
	Not Significant
IL	Influential Learning

G6

G6

R#	Mazzanine
1	1540
2	222 x 10
3	239 x 10
4	309 x 10
5	428 x 10
6	975 x 100
7	1011 x 100
8	243
9	202
10	417
11	207 x 10
12	48
13	939
14	706
15	1185
16	233 x 10
17	1577
18	953 x 100

SUMMARY OF ALL THREE EXPERIMENTS

Experiments	Variables											
	Room Size	Room Shape	Surface Reflectance	Number of Sources of Luminance	Location of Sources of Luminance	Luminance of the entry field of view (X and Y Axis)	Luminance of the entry field of view (Z axis)	Observer Location and Line of Sight	Size of Aperture	Frequency of Luminaires	Contrast	Color of Surfaces
Test Facility									IL		IL	
Three D Model North				IL					IL			
Three D Model South				IL					IL			
Three D Model East				IL					IL			
Three D Model West				IL					IL			
In Site Experiment A								IL				
In Site Experiment C					IL			IL		IL	IL	IL
In Site Experiment D					IL			IL			IL	IL
In Site Experiment E												
In Site Experiment F									IL		IL	
In Site Experiment G												

Color Key	
	Significant
	Less Significant
	Not Significant
IL	Influential Learning

VI. Conclusion

This work began with an initial strong assumption: The conviction that the amount of light in a given space could be quantified to achieve optimal perceptual results. The study, however, concluded that the most applicable recommendation is that the amount of light in a given space must be **designed** to achieve optimal results.

Some of the findings of this study include:

1. Daylight design is a sophisticated, mature and fairly developed field. It remains however, underdeveloped in arid climates, and in particular, the Arabian Gulf. Architects and designers are not participants in this dialogue bringing their learning and understanding of their respective climates and challenges to the debate.
2. Human perception is a subjective and therefore a non-quantifiable variable. The interviews at the test facility in Kuwait are indicative of one central finding: That spatial threshold is an effective way to help the eye naturally adjust to its physiological needs as it responds to a different environment.
3. Computer simulated models that study the amount of light for given spaces should be used more as references and benchmarks, as opposed to absolute requirements. This is particularly true in arid climates. For lighting design to be successful and effective, it must be tested by humans. For the space to have optimal results, it has to be experienced.
4. Design should offer more autonomy to control the amount of artificial / daylight needs dependent on the task or the activity. Uniform light distribution can overwhelm the eye as opposed to stimulate it, becoming an actual cause of strain.

5. Though the discussions with Emirates Green Building Council which are in the process of customizing LEED to be more suitable for the UAE are still at the initial stage, following their work will be integral in understanding how the climatic conditions of the Gulf find their way into building codes and municipal requirements. There is great potential here to study implications of these changes and run more thorough cost benefits analysis.

The following elements are important for designers to consider:

- The study of the lighting threshold
- The situation of lighting sources as mechanisms to stimulate the eyes
- The aperture size in buildings of arid climates to increase its visual effectiveness
- The re-evaluation of the façade design to frame views and control daylighting
- The understanding of human perception to enhance the spatial experience within built environments

VII. Acknowledgements

I owe a debt of gratitude to Professor Michelle Addington who tirelessly encouraged me to refine and sharpen both my focus and resolve. I also hold great respect for Professor Hashim Sarkis and Professor Ken Kao for their guidance and insight.

Joaquin Perez Goicoechea and Mohammed Al Sayer are my closest of friends. Through humour, encouragement, and determination, they never stopped supporting me. I wish them and their families only the best.

My family and in particular, my parents have seen me through the best and the worst of times. Without them, I am certain this work could not have been completed.

VIII. References

Bibliography

Books:

Augustesen, Christina, Ulrike Brandi, Udo Dietrich, Annette Friederici, Christoph Geissmar-Brandi, Peter Thule Kristensen, Merete Madsen, Anja Storch, and Bukhard Wand. "Lighting Design: Principles Implementation Case Studies". Munich: Birkhauser, 2006.

Benya, James, Lisa Heschong, Terry McGowan, Naomi Miller, and Francis Rubinstein. "Advanced Lighting Guidelines". California: New Buildings Institute, Inc., 2003.

Bruce, Vicki, and Patrick R. Green. "Visual Perception: Physiology, Psychology, and Ecology". 2nd ed. Hillsdale: Lawrence Erilbaum Associates, 1991.

Camody, John, Stephen Selkowitz, Eleanor S. Lee, Dariush Arasteh, and Todd Willmert. "Window Systems for High-Performance Buildings". New York: W.W. Norton & Company, 2004.

Gregory, Richard L. "Eye and Brain: the Phsychology of Seeing". 5th ed. Princeton Science Library, 1997.

Koster, Helmut. "Dynamic Daylighting Architecture, Basics, Systems, Projects". Birkhauser.

Lam, William M.C. "Perception and Lighting as Formgivers for Architecture". New York: McGraw-Hill, Inc, 1977.

Levine, Michael W., and Jeremy M. Shefner. "Fundamentals of Sensation and Perception". 2nd ed. California: Brooks/Publishing Company, 1991.

Livingstone, Margaret. "Vision and Art: The Biology of Seeing". China: Harry N. Abrams, Inc.,2002.

Michel, Lou. "Light: the Shape of Space, Designing with Space and Light". Canada: John Wiley & Sons, Inc., 1996.

Rea, Mark S. "The Lesna Lighting Handbook Reference & Application". 9th ed. The Lighting Society.

Waldman, Gary. "Introduction to Light: The Physics of Light, Vision and Color". Canada" Dover Publications, Inc. 2002.

Articles:

Aboulnaga, Mohsen M., and Yasser H. Elsheshtawy. "Environmental Sustainability Assessment of Buildings in Hot Climates: the Case If the UAE." Pergamon-Renewable Energy (2001).

Addington, Michelle. "No Building is an Island." Harvard Design Magazine 2007

Ferwerda, James A., Summanta N. Pattanaik, Peter Shirley, and Donald P. Greenberg. "A Model of Visual Adaptation for Realistic Image Synthesis". Cornell University Program of Computer Graphics (1996).

Greenberg, Donald P., Kenneth Torrance, Peter Shirley, James Arvo, James A. Ferwerda, Sumanta Pattanaik, Eric Lafortune, Bruce Walter, Sing-Choong Foo, and Ben Trumbore. "A Framwork for Realistic Image Synthesis." Cornell University Program of Computer Graphics (1997).

Haggag, M A. "Building Skin and Energy Efficiency in a Hot Climate with Particular Reference to Dubai, UAE." WIT Transactions on Ecology and the Environment 15 (2007).

Kazim, Ayoub M. "Assessments of Primary Energy Consumption and Its Environmental Consequences in the United Arab Emirates." ScienceDirect (2005).

Lee, E.S., and S.E. Selkowitz. "The New York Times Headquarters Daylighting Mockup: Monitored Performance of the Daylight Control System." Energy and Building (2005).

Loftness, Vivian, Volker Hartkopf, Beran Gurtekin, Ying Hua, Ming Qu, Megan Snyder, Yun Gu, and Xiaodi Yang. "Building Investment Decision Support, Cost-Benefit Tool to Promote Hugh Performance Components, Flexible Infrastructures and Systems Integration for Sustainable Commercial Buildings and Productive Organizations." Carnegie Mellon University Center for Building Performance and Diagnostics.

Miller, Herman. "Vision and the Computerized Office." (2001).

Office Tenant Needs Study. Center for the Built Environment. CBE, 1999. 1-11.

Pattanaik, Sumanta N., Mark D. Fairchild, James A. Ferwerda, and Donald P. Greenberg. "Multiscale Model of Adaptation, Spatial Vision and Color Appearance." Cornell University Program of Computer Graphics (1998).

Pattanaik, Sumanta N., Jack Tumblin, Hector Yee, and Donald P. Greenberg. "Time-Dependent Visual Adaptation for Fast Realistic Display." Cornell University Program of Computer Graphics (2000).

Pattanaik, Sumanta N., Jack Tumblin, Donald P. Greenberg, and Mark D. Fairchild. "A Multicale Model for Adaptation and Spatial Vision for Realistic Image Display." Cornell University Program of Computer Graphics (1998).

Tiller, D K., and J A. Veitch. "Percieved Room Brightness: Pilot Study on the Effect of Luminance Distribution." Lighting Research & Technology (1995): 93-101.

Van Bommel, Ir W J M, and Ir G J Van Den Beld. "Lighting for Work: Visual and Biological Effects." Philips Lighting (2003).

"Windows and Offices: a Study of Office Worker Performance and the Indoor Environment." Heschong Mahone Group (2003).

Online:

"Energy Consumption by Sector 2005." International Energy Association (2005)

"Climate and Atmosphere." Earth Trends. Fall 2006 <http://earthtrends.wri.org/>.

VIII. References

Appendix

Contact Information for Interviewees:

Marwa Abulhasan

Female

Age 25

Dentist

Tel. +9657315445

Mohamed Abulhasan

Male

Age 22

Financial Analyst

Tel. +9659418969

Mohammed Bader

Male

Age 30

Banker

Tel. +9656614344

Muthla Al Sayer

Female

Age 31

IT Director

Tel. +9659063828

Betool Hashem

Female

Age 58

Housewife

Tel. +9656656682

Bader AbdelKareem

Male

Age 60

Engineer

Tel. +9659067169

AbdelKareem Abdulah

Male

Age 80

Businessman

Tel. +9652573113 – Note: Interview conducted in Arabic through Nasser AbulHasan

Futooh Mousa

Female

Age 78

Housewife

Tel. +9652573113 – Note: Interview conducted in Arabic through Nasser AbulHasan

Joaquin Perez-Goicoechea

Male

Age 36

Architect

Tel. +34630831396

Lamis Ibrahim

Female

Age 25

Accountant

Tel. +19176574030

MARWA ABDULHASSAN

Questionnaire
Part 1

Instructions

We would like you to answer the following survey. Please fill out this questionnaire as completely as possible. Please respond to all of the items as openly and as honestly as possible. Try to answer all the questions based on your immediate impression. There is no right or wrong answer: it is only your interpretation that is important.

Part A: Background Information

1. Today's Date ______ June 21st, 2005
   Start Time ______ 12 PM

2. What is your gender?
   a. Male
   (b.) Female

3. How old are you?
   (a.) Under 40 years old
   b. 40 or over

4. Do you wear glasses at work?
   a. Yes
   (b.) No

5. Do you have any eye conditions that would affect your overall perception (cataracts, sensitivities to light, allergies etc.)
   a. Yes
   (b.) No

MA

6. Please assign a rating from 1 to 5 for what you feel is important of the following items to create a pleasant and productive office environment. Number 1 being the least important and 5, the most.

Item	**Rating Unimportant**			**Very Important**	
a. Good temperature	1	2	3	4	(5)
b. Good lighting	1	2	3	(4)	5
c. Windows	1	2	3	4	(5)
d. A View	1	2	3	4	(5)
e. comfortable furniture	1	2	3	4	(5)
f. no noise	1	2	3	4	(5)
g. controllable lights or shades	1	2	3	(4)	5
h. An attractive environment	1	2	3	(4)	5
i. a good monitor	1	2	3	(4)	5

7. Please assign a rating from 1 to 5 for your sensitivity to the following items, with 1 being the least important and 5 being the most important.

Item	**Rating Unimportant**			**Very Important**	
a. Glare	1	2	(3)	4	5
b. Cold	1	2	3	4	(5)
c. Heat	1	2	3	4	(5)
d. Gloominess	1	(2)	3	4	5
e. Noise	1	2	3	(4)	5
f. Visual distractions	1	2	(3)	4	5

MMA

8. When you perform your work tasks, what is your preferred light level in your workspace?

	Very low	low	Moderate	Bright	Very Bright
Light Level	1	2	(3)	4	5

Any Comments:

With my profession as being a dentist, lighting is an important factor in my practice.

MA

Questionnaire
Part 2

Experiment A
Size of Opening: 50cmX100cm

Name of Interviewee:

MARWA ABULHASSAN

Part B: Entering the Box

1. How do you feel as you enter the room?

   DARK and HOT

2. What do you see?

   DESK and a CHAIR

3. Are you comfortable?

   NOT REALLY

Part C: Sitting at the Desk

1. Can you see me clearly?

   YES

2. Can you read the newspaper on the desk?

   YES

3. Do you want to switch an artificial light?

   I WOULD LIKE TOO, BUT THERE IS NO NEED

4. Do you want to open a window?

   NO

5. Do you want to have a view?

   YES

Part D: Exiting the Box

1. How do you feel as soon as you leave the room?

   BRIGHT

MA

Questionnaire
Part 2

Experiment B
Size of Opening: 100cmX100cm

Name of Interviewee:

MARWA ABULHASSAN

Part B: Entering the Box

4. How do you feel as you enter the room?

SAME

5. What do you see?

DESK and a CHAIR

6. Are you comfortable?

NO

Part C: Sitting at the Desk

6. Can you see me clearly?

YES

7. Can you read the newspaper on the desk?

YES

8. Do you want to switch an artificial light?

I WOULD LIKE TOO BUT THERE IS NO NEED

9. Do you want to open a window?

NO

10. Do you want to have a view?

YES

Part D: Exiting the Box

2. How do you feel as soon as you leave the room?

BRIGHT

MA

Questionnaire
Part 2

Experiment C
Size of Opening: 200cmX200cm

Name of Interviewee:

MARWA ABULHASSAN

Part B: Entering the Box

7. How do you feel as you enter the room?

   SAME

8. What do you see?

   DESK and a CHAIR

9. Are you comfortable?

   NO

Part C: Sitting at the Desk

11. Can you see me clearly?

    YES

12. Can you read the newspaper on the desk?

    YES

13. Do you want to switch an artificial light?

    I WOULD LIKE TOO BUT THERE IS NO NEED

14. Do you want to open a window?

    NO

15. Do you want to have a view?

    YES

Part D: Exiting the Box

3. How do you feel as soon as you leave the room?

   BRIGHT

Questionnaire
Part 1

Instructions

We would like you to answer the following survey. Please fill out this questionnaire as completely as possible. Please respond to all of the items as openly and as honestly as possible. Try to answer all the questions based on your immediate impression. There is no right or wrong answer: it is only your interpretation that is important.

Part A: Background Information

1. Today's Date 24/06/05
   Start Time 12.30 PM

2. What is your gender?
   a. Male (circled)
   b. Female

3. How old are you?
   a. Under 40 years old (circled)
   b. 40 or over

4. Do you wear glasses at work?
   a. Yes (circled)
   b. No

5. Do you have any eye conditions that would affect your overall perception (cataracts, sensitivities to light, allergies etc.)
   a. Yes (circled)
   b. No

MBA

6. Please assign a rating from 1 to 5 for what you feel is important of the following items to create a pleasant and productive office environment. Number 1 being the least important and 5, the most.

Item	Rating Unimportant				Very Important
a. Good temperature	1	(2)	(3)	4	5
b. Good lighting	1	2	(3)	4	5
c. Windows	1	2	(3)	4	5
d. A View	1	2	3	4	(5)
e. comfortable furniture	1	2	(3)	4	5
f. no noise	1	2	(3)	4	5
g. controllable lights or shades	1	2	(3)	4	5
h. An attractive environment	1	2	(3)	4	5
i. a good monitor	1	2	3	(4)	5

7. Please assign a rating from 1 to 5 for your sensitivity to the following items, with 1 being the least important and 5 being the most important.

Item	Rating Unimportant				Very Important
a. Glare	1	(2)	3	4	5
b. Cold	1	(2)	3	4	5
c. Heat	1	(2)	3	4	5
d. Gloominess	1	(2)	3	4	5
e. Noise	1	(2)	3	4	5
f. Visual distractions	1	(2)	3	4	5

8. When you perform your work tasks, what is your preferred light level in your workspace?

	Very low	low	Moderate	Bright	Very Bright
Light Level	1	2	(3)	4	5

Any Comments:

MBA

Questionnaire
Part 2

Experiment A
Size of Opening: 50cmX100cm

Name of Interviewee:

Mohammad Abulhassan

Part B: Entering the Box

1. How do you feel as you enter the room?

   humid, hot
2. What do you see?

   table
3. Are you comfortable?

   no

Part C: Sitting at the Desk

1. Can you see me clearly?

   yes
2. Can you read the newspaper on the desk?

   yes
3. Do you want to switch an artificial light?

   yes
4. Do you want to open a window?

   yes
5. Do you want to have a view?

   no

Part D: Exiting the Box

1. How do you feel as soon as you leave the room?

   fine

Questionnaire
Part 2

Experiment B
Size of Opening: 100cmX100cm

Name of Interviewee:

Mohammad Abulhassan

Part B: Entering the Box

4. How do you feel as you enter the room?

   humid, hot

5. What do you see?

   table

6. Are you comfortable?

   no

Part C: Sitting at the Desk

6. Can you see me clearly?

   yes

7. Can you read the newspaper on the desk?

   yes

8. Do you want to switch an artificial light?

   yes

9. Do you want to open a window?

   yes

10. Do you want to have a view?

    no

Part D: Exiting the Box

2. How do you feel as soon as you leave the room?

   fine

MBA

Questionnaire
Part 2

Experiment C
Size of Opening: 200cmX200cm

Name of Interviewee:

Mohammad Abulhassan

Part B: Entering the Box

7. How do you feel as you enter the room?

humid, hot

8. What do you see?

table

9. Are you comfortable?

no

Part C: Sitting at the Desk

11. Can you see me clearly?

yes

12. Can you read the newspaper on the desk?

yes

13. Do you want to switch an artificial light?

yes

14. Do you want to open a window?

yes

15. Do you want to have a view?

no

Part D: Exiting the Box

3. How do you feel as soon as you leave the room?

fine

mBS

Questionnaire
Part 1

Instructions

We would like you to answer the following survey. Please fill out this questionnaire as completely as possible. Please respond to all of the items as openly and as honestly as possible. Try to answer all the questions based on your immediate impression. There is no right or wrong answer: it is only your interpretation that is important.

Part A: Background Information

1. Today's Date — 21/6/2005
   Start Time — 1 PM

2. What is your gender?
   a. Male ✓
   b. Female

3. How old are you?
   a. Under 40 years old ✓
   b. 40 or over

4. Do you wear glasses at work?
   a. Yes ✓
   b. No

5. Do you have any eye conditions that would affect your overall perception (cataracts, sensitivities to light, allergies etc.)
   a. Yes
   b. No ✓

MBS

6. Please assign a rating from 1 to 5 for what you feel is important of the following items to create a pleasant and productive office environment. Number 1 being the least important and 5, the most.

Item	**Rating** **Unimportant**				**Very Important**
a. Good temperature	1	2	3	4	5
b. Good lighting	1	2	3	4	5
c. Windows	1	2	3	4	5
d. A View	1	2	3	4	5
e. comfortable furniture	1	2	3	4	5
f. no noise	1	2	3	4	5
g. controllable lights or shades	1	2	3	4	5
h. An attractive environment	1	2	3	4	5
i. a good monitor	1	2	3	4	5

7. Please assign a rating from 1 to 5 for your sensitivity to the following items, with 1 being the least important and 5 being the most important.

Item	**Rating** **Unimportant**				**Very Important**
a. Glare	1	2	3	4	5
b. Cold	1	2	3	4	5
c. Heat	1	2	3	4	5
d. Gloominess	1	2	3	4	5
e. Noise	1	2	3	4	5
f. Visual distractions	1	2	3	4	5

MBS

8. When you perform your work tasks, what is your preferred light level in your workspace?

	Very low	low	Moderate	Bright	Very Bright
Light Level	1	2	3	4 (circled)	5

Any Comments:

view is very important for me as I have clients

MBS

Questionnaire
Part 2

Experiment A
Size of Opening: 50cmX100cm

Name of Interviewee:

Mohammad Bader

Part B: Entering the Box

1. How do you feel as you enter the room?

   Nothing

2. What do you see?

   Desk

3. Are you comfortable?

   No

Part C: Sitting at the Desk

1. Can you see me clearly?

   Yes

2. Can you read the newspaper on the desk?

   Yes

3. Do you want to switch an artificial light?

   Yes

4. Do you want to open a window?

   Yes

5. Do you want to have a view?

   Yes

Part D: Exiting the Box

1. How do you feel as soon as you leave the room?

   Sunny

MBS

Questionnaire
Part 2

Experiment B
Size of Opening: 100cmX100cm

Name of Interviewee:

Mohammad Bader

Part B: Entering the Box

4. How do you feel as you enter the room?

Nothing

5. What do you see?

Desk

6. Are you comfortable?

No

Part C: Sitting at the Desk

6. Can you see me clearly?

Yes

7. Can you read the newspaper on the desk?

Yes

8. Do you want to switch an artificial light?

Yes

9. Do you want to open a window?

Yes

10. Do you want to have a view?

Yes

Part D: Exiting the Box

2. How do you feel as soon as you leave the room?

Sunny

MBS

Questionnaire
Part 2

Experiment C
Size of Opening: 200cmX200cm

Name of Interviewee:

Mohammad Bader

Part B: Entering the Box

7. How do you feel as you enter the room?

   Nothing

8. What do you see?

   Desk

9. Are you comfortable?

   No

Part C: Sitting at the Desk

11. Can you see me clearly?

    Yes

12. Can you read the newspaper on the desk?

    Yes

13. Do you want to switch an artificial light?

    Yes

14. Do you want to open a window?

    Yes

15. Do you want to have a view?

    Yes

Part D: Exiting the Box

3. How do you feel as soon as you leave the room?

   Sunny

MS

Questionnaire
Part 1

Instructions

We would like you to answer the following survey. Please fill out this questionnaire as completely as possible. Please respond to all of the items as openly and as honestly as possible. Try to answer all the questions based on your immediate impression. There is no right or wrong answer: it is only your interpretation that is important.

Part A: Background Information

1. Today's Date — June 21, 2005
   Start Time — 1:00 p.m.
2. What is your gender?
   a. Male
   b. Female — b
3. How old are you?
   a. Under 40 years old — a
   b. 40 or over
4. Do you wear glasses at work?
   a. Yes
   b. No — b
5. Do you have any eye conditions that would affect your overall perception (cataracts, sensitivities to light, allergies etc.)
   a. Yes
   b. No — b

6. Please assign a rating from 1 to 5 for what you feel is important of the following items to create a pleasant and productive office environment. Number 1 being the least important and 5, the most.

Item	**Rating** **Unimportant**			**Very Important**	
a. Good temperature	1	2	3	4	5
b. Good lighting	1	2	3	4	5
c. Windows	1	2	3	4	5
d. A View	1	2	3	4	5
e. comfortable furniture	1	2	3	4	5
f. no noise	1	2	3	4	5
g. controllable lights or shades	1	2	3	4	5
h. An attractive environment	1	2	3	4	5
i. a good monitor	1	2	3	4	5

7. Please assign a rating from 1 to 5 for your sensitivity to the following items, with 1 being the least important and 5 being the most important.

Item	**Rating** **Unimportant**			**Very Important**	
a. Glare	1	2	3	4	5
b. Cold	1	2	3	4	5
c. Heat	1	2	3	4	5
d. Gloominess	1	2	3	4	5
e. Noise	1	2	3	4	5
f. Visual distractions	1	2	3	4	5

MS

8. When you perform your work tasks, what is your preferred light level in your workspace?

	Very low	low	Moderate	Bright	Very Bright
Light Level	1	2	(3)	4	5

Any Comments:

I prefer natural sunlight.

MS

Light, Sight and Architecture

An approach to designing for the optimum by capturing the minimum

Questionnaire
Part 2

Experiment A
Size of Opening: 50cmX100cm

Name of Interviewee:
Muthla Al Sayer

Part B: Entering the Box

1. How do you feel as you enter the room?
   Hot and uneasy
2. What do you see?
   a desk, chair, and a small window
3. Are you comfortable?
   No

Part C: Sitting at the Desk

1. Can you see me clearly?
   yes
2. Can you read the newspaper on the desk?
   yes
3. Do you want to switch an artificial light?
   No
4. Do you want to open a window?
   yes
5. Do you want to have a view?
   yes

Part D: Exiting the Box

1. How do you feel as soon as you leave the room?
   Relieved

115

Questionnaire
Part 2

Experiment B
Size of Opening: 100cmX100cm

Name of Interviewee:
Mutlla Al Sayer

Part B: Entering the Box

4. How do you feel as you enter the room?
   Hot and uneasy
5. What do you see?
   a desk, chair, and a window
6. Are you comfortable?
   No

Part C: Sitting at the Desk

6. Can you see me clearly?
   yes
7. Can you read the newspaper on the desk?
   yes
8. Do you want to switch an artificial light?
   No
9. Do you want to open a window?
   yes
10. Do you want to have a view?
   yes

Part D: Exiting the Box

2. How do you feel as soon as you leave the room?
   Relieved

MS

Questionnaire
Part 2

Experiment C
Size of Opening: 200cmX200cm

Name of Interviewee:
Mutlla Al Sayer

Part B: Entering the Box

7. How do you feel as you enter the room?
Hot

8. What do you see?
a desk, chair, and a big window

9. Are you comfortable?
Yes

Part C: Sitting at the Desk

11. Can you see me clearly?
Yes

12. Can you read the newspaper on the desk?
Yes

13. Do you want to switch an artificial light?
NO

14. Do you want to open a window?
Yes

15. Do you want to have a view?
No

Part D: Exiting the Box

3. How do you feel as soon as you leave the room?
O.K.

BH

Questionnaire
Part 1

Instructions

We would like you to answer the following survey. Please fill out this questionnaire as completely as possible. Please respond to all of the items as openly and as honestly as possible. Try to answer all the questions based on your immediate impression. There is no right or wrong answer: it is only your interpretation that is important.

Part A: Background Information

1. Today's Date — June 21, 2005
   Start Time — 1.30 pm

2. What is your gender? — b
   a. Male
   b. Female

3. How old are you? — b
   a. Under 40 years old
   b. 40 or over

4. Do you wear glasses at work? — a
   a. Yes
   b. No

5. Do you have any eye conditions that would affect your overall perception (cataracts, sensitivities to light, allergies etc.) — a
   a. Yes
   b. No

6. Please assign a rating from 1 to 5 for what you feel is important of the following items to create a pleasant and productive office environment. Number 1 being the least important and 5, the most.

Item	Rating Unimportant				Very Important
a. Good temperature	1	2	3	4	5
b. Good lighting	1	2	3	4	5
c. Windows	1	2	3	4	5
d. A View	1	2	3	4	5
e. comfortable furniture	1	2	3	4	5
f. no noise	1	2	3	4	5
g. controllable lights or shades	1	2	3	4	5
h. An attractive environment	1	2	3	4	5
i. a good monitor	1	2	3	4	5

7. Please assign a rating from 1 to 5 for your sensitivity to the following items, with 1 being the least important and 5 being the most important.

Item	Rating Unimportant				Very Important
a. Glare	1	2	3	4	5
b. Cold	1	2	3	4	5
c. Heat	1	2	3	4	5
d. Gloominess	1	2	3	4	5
e. Noise	1	2	3	4	5
f. Visual distractions	1	2	3	4	5

8. When you perform your work tasks, what is your preferred light level in your workspace?

	Very low	low	Moderate	Bright	Very Bright
Light Level	1	2	3	4	5

Any Comments: —

B14

Questionnaire
Part 2

Experiment A
Size of Opening: 50cmX100cm

Name of Interviewee:
Betool Hashim

Part B: Entering the Box

1. How do you feel as you enter the room?
   It's humid & dark
2. What do you see?
   a desk, a chair, and a window
3. Are you comfortable?
   No

Part C: Sitting at the Desk

1. Can you see me clearly?
   Yes
2. Can you read the newspaper on the desk?
   No
3. Do you want to switch an artificial light?
   Yes
4. Do you want to open a window?
   No
5. Do you want to have a view?
   Yes

Part D: Exiting the Box

1. How do you feel as soon as you leave the room?
   It is brighter on the outside

B12

Questionnaire
Part 2

Experiment B
Size of Opening: 100cmX100cm

Name of Interviewee:
Betool Hashim

Part B: Entering the Box

4. How do you feel as you enter the room?
   Its Humid & dark
5. What do you see?
   a desk, a chair, and a window
6. Are you comfortable?
   No

Part C: Sitting at the Desk

6. Can you see me clearly?
   Yes
7. Can you read the newspaper on the desk?
   With discomfort
8. Do you want to switch an artificial light?
   Yes
9. Do you want to open a window?
   No
10. Do you want to have a view?
    Yes

Part D: Exiting the Box

2. How do you feel as soon as you leave the room?
   It seems brighter on the outside

BH

Questionnaire
Part 2

Experiment C
Size of Opening: 200cmX200cm

Name of Interviewee:
Betool Hashim

Part B: Entering the Box

7. How do you feel as you enter the room?
   Humid
8. What do you see?
   a desk, a chair, and a window
9. Are you comfortable?
   No

Part C: Sitting at the Desk

11. Can you see me clearly?
    Yes
12. Can you read the newspaper on the desk?
    Yes
13. Do you want to switch an artificial light?
    No
14. Do you want to open a window?
    No
15. Do you want to have a view?
    Yes

Part D: Exiting the Box

3. How do you feel as soon as you leave the room?
   It seems brighter on the outside

BA

Questionnaire
Part 1

Instructions

We would like you to answer the following survey. Please fill out this questionnaire as completely as possible. Please respond to all of the items as openly and as honestly as possible. Try to answer all the questions based on your immediate impression. There is no right or wrong answer: it is only your interpretation that is important.

Part A: Background Information

1. Today's Date — June 21st, 2005
   Start Time — 1:45pm

2. What is your gender?
   a. Male (circled)
   b. Female

3. How old are you?
   a. Under 40 years old
   b. 40 or over (circled)

4. Do you wear glasses at work?
   a. Yes (circled)
   b. No

5. Do you have any eye conditions that would affect your overall perception (cataracts, sensitivities to light, allergies etc.)
   a. Yes (circled)
   b. No

BA

6. Please assign a rating from 1 to 5 for what you feel is important of the following items to create a pleasant and productive office environment. Number 1 being the least important and 5, the most.

Item	Rating Unimportant				Very Important
a. Good temperature	1	2	3	4	5
b. Good lighting	1	2	3	4	5
c. Windows	1	2	3	4	5
d. A View	1	2	3	4	5
e. comfortable furniture	1	2	3	4	5
f. no noise	1	2	3	4	5
g. controllable lights or shades	1	2	3	4	5
h. An attractive environment	1	2	3	4	5
i. a good monitor	1	2	3	4	5

7. Please assign a rating from 1 to 5 for your sensitivity to the following items, with 1 being the least important and 5 being the most important.

Item	Rating Unimportant				Very Important
a. Glare	1	2	3	4	5
b. Cold	1	2	3	4	5
c. Heat	1	2	3	4	5
d. Gloominess	1	2	3	4	5
e. Noise	1	2	3	4	5
f. Visual distractions	1	2	3	4	5

BA

8. When you perform your work tasks, what is your preferred light level in your workspace?

	Very low	low	Moderate	Bright	Very Bright
Light Level	1	2	3	(4)	5

Any Comments:
As a contractor, light is very important to perform at the best levels.

BA

Light, Sight and Architecture

An approach to designing for the optimum by capturing the minimum

Questionnaire
Part 2

Experiment A
Size of Opening: 50cmX100cm

Name of Interviewee:

Badr Abdelkareem

Part B: Entering the Box

1. How do you feel as you enter the room?
   closed in and restricted
2. What do you see?
   furniture
3. Are you comfortable?
   no

Part C: Sitting at the Desk

1. Can you see me clearly?
   yes
2. Can you read the newspaper on the desk?
   yes
3. Do you want to switch an artificial light?
   yes
4. Do you want to open a window?
   yes
5. Do you want to have a view?
   no

Part D: Exiting the Box

1. How do you feel as soon as you leave the room?
   relieved !

BA

Light, Sight and Architecture

An approach to designing for the optimum by capturing the minimum

Questionnaire
Part 2

Experiment B
Size of Opening: 100cmX100cm

Name of Interviewee:

Badr Abdelkareem

Part B: Entering the Box

4. How do you feel as you enter the room?

 restricted

5. What do you see?

 furniture

6. Are you comfortable?

 no

Part C: Sitting at the Desk

6. Can you see me clearly?

 yes

7. Can you read the newspaper on the desk?

 yes

8. Do you want to switch an artificial light?

 yes

9. Do you want to open a window?

 yes

10. Do you want to have a view?

 no

Part D: Exiting the Box

2. How do you feel as soon as you leave the room?

 more relaxed.

BA

Questionnaire
Part 2

Experiment C
Size of Opening: 200cmX200cm

Name of Interviewee:

Badr Abdelkareem

Part B: Entering the Box

7. How do you feel as you enter the room?
   restricted and uncomfortable
8. What do you see?
   desk/chair
9. Are you comfortable?
   no

Part C: Sitting at the Desk

11. Can you see me clearly?
    yes
12. Can you read the newspaper on the desk?
    yes
13. Do you want to switch an artificial light?
    yes
14. Do you want to open a window?
    yes
15. Do you want to have a view?
    no

Part D: Exiting the Box

3. How do you feel as soon as you leave the room?
   relaxed

FM

Light, Sight and Architecture

An approach to designing for the optimum by capturing the minimum

Questionnaire
Part 1

Instructions

We would like you to answer the following survey. Please fill out this questionnaire as completely as possible. Please respond to all of the items as openly and as honestly as possible. Try to answer all the questions based on your immediate impression. There is no right or wrong answer: it is only your interpretation that is important.

Part A: Background Information

1. Today's Date — June 22 2005
   Start Time

2. What is your gender?
   a. Male
   b. Female (circled)

3. How old are you?
   a. Under 40 years old
   b. 40 or over (circled) — 78

4. Do you wear glasses at work? — when reading / Do not work
   a. Yes (circled)
   b. No

5. Do you have any eye conditions that would affect your overall perception (cataracts, sensitivities to light, allergies etc.)
   a. Yes (circled)
   b. No

6. Please assign a rating from 1 to 5 for what you feel is important of the following items to create a pleasant and productive office environment. Number 1 being the least important and 5, the most.

Item	Rating Unimportant			Very Important	
a. Good temperature	1	2	3	4	5
b. Good lighting	1	2	3	4	5
c. Windows	1	2	3	4	5
d. A View	1	2	3	4	5
e. comfortable furniture	1	2	3	4	5
f. no noise	1	2	3	4	5
g. controllable lights or shades	1	2	3	4	5
h. An attractive environment	1	2	3	4	5
i. a good monitor	1	2	3	4	5

7. Please assign a rating from 1 to 5 for your sensitivity to the following items, with 1 being the least important and 5 being the most important.

Item	Rating Unimportant			Very Important	
a. Glare	1	2	3	4	5
b. Cold	1	2	3	4	5
c. Heat	1	2	3	4	5
d. Gloominess	1	2	3	4	5
e. Noise	1	2	3	4	5
f. Visual distractions	1	2	3	4	5

FM

8. When you perform your work tasks, what is your preferred light level in your workspace?

	Very low	low	Moderate	Bright	Very Bright
Light Level	1	2	3	4	(5)

Any Comments:

need good view and a lot of natural light

FM

Questionnaire
Part 2

Experiment A
Size of Opening: 50cmX100cm

Name of Interviewee:

Part B: Entering the Box

1. How do you feel as you enter the room?
   not comfortable
2. What do you see?
   table 1 and open window
3. Are you comfortable?
   no

Part C: Sitting at the Desk

1. Can you see me clearly?
   yes
2. Can you read the newspaper on the desk?
   yes
3. Do you want to switch an artificial light?
   yes
4. Do you want to open a window?
   no
5. Do you want to have a view?
   yes

Part D: Exiting the Box

1. How do you feel as soon as you leave the room?
   bright, hot

FM

Light, Sight and Architecture

An approach to designing for the optimum by capturing the minimum

Questionnaire
Part 2

Experiment B
Size of Opening: 100cmX100cm

Name of Interviewee:

Part B: Entering the Box

4. How do you feel as you enter the room?

 not comfortable

5. What do you see?

 same

6. Are you comfortable?

 no

Part C: Sitting at the Desk

6. Can you see me clearly?

 yes

7. Can you read the newspaper on the desk?

 yes

8. Do you want to switch an artificial light?

 yes

9. Do you want to open a window?

 no, but it could be good

10. Do you want to have a view?

 yes

Part D: Exiting the Box

2. How do you feel as soon as you leave the room?

 same

HM

Questionnaire
Part 2

Experiment C
Size of Opening: 200cmX200cm

Name of Interviewee:

Part B: Entering the Box

7. How do you feel as you enter the room?
   ok, but still not comfortable
8. What do you see?
   table and open window
9. Are you comfortable?
   no

Part C: Sitting at the Desk

11. Can you see me clearly?
    yes
12. Can you read the newspaper on the desk?
    yes
13. Do you want to switch an artificial light?
    yes
14. Do you want to open a window?
    No
15. Do you want to have a view?
    yes

Part D: Exiting the Box

3. How do you feel as soon as you leave the room?
   bright, hot

AAH

Light, Sight and Architecture

An approach to designing for the optimum by capturing the minimum

Questionnaire
Part 1

Instructions

We would like you to answer the following survey. Please fill out this questionnaire as completely as possible. Please respond to all of the items as openly and as honestly as possible. Try to answer all the questions based on your immediate impression. There is no right or wrong answer: it is only your interpretation that is important.

Part A: Background Information

1. Today's Date — Jan/22/05
   Start Time — 12 pm
2. What is your gender? — Male
   a. Male
   b. Female
3. How old are you? — 80
   a. Under 40 years old
   b. 40 or over
4. Do you wear glasses at work? — Yes
   a. Yes
   b. No
5. Do you have any eye conditions that would affect your overall perception (cataracts, sensitivities to light, allergies etc.) — Yes, sensitive eye
   a. Yes
   b. No

written by Nasser Abulhasan on behalf of Abdulkareem Abdullah

AAH

6. Please assign a rating from 1 to 5 for what you feel is important of the following items to create a pleasant and productive office environment. Number 1 being the least important and 5, the most.

Item	Rating Unimportant			Very Important	
a. Good temperature	1	2	3	4	5
b. Good lighting	1	2	3	4	5
c. Windows	1	2	3	4	5
d. A View	1	2	3	4	5
e. comfortable furniture	1	2	3	4	5
f. no noise	1	2	3	4	5
g. controllable lights or shades	1	2	3	4	5
h. An attractive environment	1	2	3	4	5
i. a good monitor	1	2	3	4	5

7. Please assign a rating from 1 to 5 for your sensitivity to the following items, with 1 being the least important and 5 being the most important.

Item	Rating Unimportant			Very Important	
a. Glare	1	2	3	4	5 *not sure what is
b. Cold	1	2	3	4	5
c. Heat	1	2	3	4	5
d. Gloominess	1	2	3	4	5
e. Noise	1	2	3	4	5
f. Visual distractions	1	2	3	4	5

AAH

8. When you perform your work tasks, what is your preferred light level in your workspace?

	Very low	low	Moderate	Bright	Very Bright
Light Level	1	2	3	4	(5)

Any Comments:

All rooms have to be very bright – use florecent lighting.

AAH

Light, Sight and Architecture

An approach to designing for the optimum by capturing the minimum

Questionnaire
Part 2

Experiment A
Size of Opening: 50cmX100cm

Name of Interviewee:

Part B: Entering the Box

1. How do you feel as you enter the room?

   ok

2. What do you see?

   window and tabel / chair

3. Are you comfortable?

   no

Part C: Sitting at the Desk

1. Can you see me clearly?

   not very clear

2. Can you read the newspaper on the desk?

   no, but I see it

3. Do you want to switch an artificial light?

   yes

4. Do you want to open a window?

   yes, to bring more light

5. Do you want to have a view?

   yes, but not important

Part D: Exiting the Box

1. How do you feel as soon as you leave the room?

   very bright

AAH

Questionnaire
Part 2

Experiment B
Size of Opening: 100cmX100cm

Name of Interviewee:

Part B: Entering the Box

4. How do you feel as you enter the room?
   ok
5. What do you see?
   same
6. Are you comfortable?
   no

Part C: Sitting at the Desk

6. Can you see me clearly?
   not
7. Can you read the newspaper on the desk?
   no, but I see it well
8. Do you want to switch an artificial light?
   yes
9. Do you want to open a window?
   same
10. Do you want to have a view?
    yes

Part D: Exiting the Box

2. How do you feel as soon as you leave the room?
   ok

AAH

Light, Sight and Architecture

An approach to designing for the optimum by capturing the minimum

Questionnaire
Part 2

Experiment C
Size of Opening: 200cmX200cm

Name of Interviewee:

Part B: Entering the Box

7. How do you feel as you enter the room?

   ok

8. What do you see?

   same

9. Are you comfortable?

   no

Part C: Sitting at the Desk

11. Can you see me clearly?

    not

12. Can you read the newspaper on the desk?

    see it, but can't read b/c small letters *

13. Do you want to switch an artificial light?

    Yes

14. Do you want to open a window?

    Same

15. Do you want to have a view?

    yes

Part D: Exiting the Box

3. How do you feel as soon as you leave the room?

   bright, ok

5

Questionnaire
Part 1

Instructions

We would like you to answer the following survey. Please fill out this questionnaire as completely as possible. Please respond to all of the items as openly and as honestly as possible. Try to answer all the questions based on your immediate impression. There is no right or wrong answer: it is only your interpretation that is important.

Part A: Background Information

1. Today's Date 21/06/2005
   Start Time 2 pm
2. What is your gender?
   a. Male ✓
   b. Female
3. How old are you?
   a. Under 40 years old ✓
   b. 40 or over
4. Do you wear glasses at work?
   a. Yes
   b. No ✓
5. Do you have any eye conditions that would affect your overall perception (cataracts, sensitivities to light, allergies etc.)
   a. Yes
   b. No ✓

6. Please assign a rating from 1 to 5 for what you feel is important of the following items to create a pleasant and productive office environment. Number 1 being the least important and 5, the most.

Item	Rating Unimportant				Very Important
a. Good temperature	1	2	3	4	(5)
b. Good lighting	1	2	3	4	(5)
c. Windows	1	2	3	4	(5)
d. A View	1	2	3	4	(5)
e. comfortable furniture	1	2	3	4	(5)
f. no noise	1	2	3	(4)	5
g. controllable lights or shades	1	2	3	4	(5)
h. An attractive environment	1	2	3	(4)	5
i. a good monitor	1	2	3	4	(5)

7. Please assign a rating from 1 to 5 for your sensitivity to the following items, with 1 being the least important and 5 being the most important.

Item	Rating Unimportant				Very Important
a. Glare	1	(2)	3	4	5
b. Cold	1	(2)	3	4	5
c. Heat	1	2	(3)	4	5
d. Gloominess	1	(2)	3	4	5
e. Noise	1	2	(3)	4	5
f. Visual distractions	1	2	(3)	4	5

8. When you perform your work tasks, what is your preferred light level in your workspace?

	Very low	low	Moderate	Bright	Very Bright
Light Level	1	2	3	4	(5)

Any Comments:

LIGHT IS CRUCIAL !

Questionnaire
Part 2

Experiment A
Size of Opening: 50cmX100cm

Name of Interviewee:

JOAQUIN PEREZ GOICOECHEA

Part B: Entering the Box

1. How do you feel as you enter the room?
   UNCOMFORTABLE
2. What do you see?
   TABLE, CHAIR, NEWSPAPER
3. Are you comfortable?
   NO

Part C: Sitting at the Desk

1. Can you see me clearly?
   YES
2. Can you read the newspaper on the desk?
   YES
3. Do you want to switch an artificial light?
   YES!
4. Do you want to open a window?
   YES
5. Do you want to have a view?
   YES

Part D: Exiting the Box

1. How do you feel as soon as you leave the room?
   RELAXED

Questionnaire
Part 2

Experiment B
Size of Opening: 100cmX100cm

Name of Interviewee:
JOAQUIN PEREZ GOICOECHEA

Part B: Entering the Box

4. How do you feel as you enter the room?
   UNCOMFORTABLE
5. What do you see?
   TABLE, CHAIR, NEWSPAPER
6. Are you comfortable?
   NO

Part C: Sitting at the Desk

6. Can you see me clearly?
   YES
7. Can you read the newspaper on the desk?
   YES
8. Do you want to switch an artificial light?
   YES
9. Do you want to open a window?
   YES
10. Do you want to have a view?
    YES

Part D: Exiting the Box

2. How do you feel as soon as you leave the room?
   BETTER

J

Questionnaire
Part 2

Experiment C
Size of Opening: 200cmX200cm

Name of Interviewee:
JOAQUIN PEREZ GOICOECHEA

Part B: Entering the Box

7. How do you feel as you enter the room?
UNINSPIRED, UNCOMFORTABLE
8. What do you see?
TABLE, CHAIR, NEWSPAPER
9. Are you comfortable?
NO

Part C: Sitting at the Desk

11. Can you see me clearly?
YES
12. Can you read the newspaper on the desk?
YES
13. Do you want to switch an artificial light?
YES
14. Do you want to open a window?
YES
15. Do you want to have a view?
YES

Part D: Exiting the Box

3. How do you feel as soon as you leave the room?
MORE RELAXED

Questionnaire
Part 1

Instructions

We would like you to answer the following survey. Please fill out this questionnaire as completely as possible. Please respond to all of the items as openly and as honestly as possible. Try to answer all the questions based on your immediate impression. There is no right or wrong answer: it is only your interpretation that is important.

Part A: Background Information

1. Today's Date ___June 22, 2005___
   Start Time ___2pm___

2. What is your gender?
   a. Male
   b. Female (circled)

3. How old are you? ___Sorry - 25___
   a. Under 40 years old
   b. 40 or over

4. Do you wear glasses at work? ___Yes, sometimes___
   a. Yes
   b. No

5. Do you have any eye conditions that would affect your overall perception (cataracts, sensitivities to light, allergies etc.) ___No.___
   a. Yes
   b. No

6. Please assign a rating from 1 to 5 for what you feel is important of the following items to create a pleasant and productive office environment. Number 1 being the least important and 5, the most.

Item	**Rating** **Unimportant**			**Very Important**	
a. Good temperature	1	2	3	4	5
b. Good lighting	1	2	3	4	5
c. Windows	1	2	3	4	5
d. A View	1	2	3	4	5
e. comfortable furniture	1	2	3	4	5
f. no noise	1	2	3	4	5
g. controllable lights or shades	1	2	3	4	5
h. An attractive environment	1	2	3	4	5
i. a good monitor	1	2	3	4	5

7. Please assign a rating from 1 to 5 for your sensitivity to the following items, with 1 being the least important and 5 being the most important.

Item	**Rating** **Unimportant**			**Very Important**	
a. Glare	1	2	3	4	5
b. Cold	1	2	3	4	5
c. Heat	1	2	3	4	5
d. Gloominess	1	2	3	4	5
e. Noise	1	2	3	4	5
f. Visual distractions	1	2	3	4	5

8. When you perform your work tasks, what is your preferred light level in your workspace?

	Very low	low	Moderate	Bright	Very Bright
Light Level	1	2	3	4	(5)

Any Comments:

I work long hours - light is important
but not too much. I hate
reflections on my monitor/screen
from the windows. The
shades don't always help.

Questionnaire
Part 2

Experiment A
Size of Opening: 50cmX100cm

Name of Interviewee: Lamis Ibrahim.

Part B: Entering the Box

1. How do you feel as you enter the room?
hot and dark

2. What do you see?
a table.

3. Are you comfortable?
Somewhat.

Part C: Sitting at the Desk

1. Can you see me clearly?
Yes

2. Can you read the newspaper on the desk?
Yes

3. Do you want to switch an artificial light?
Yes - of course

4. Do you want to open a window?
Yes

5. Do you want to have a view?
Yes

Part D: Exiting the Box

1. How do you feel as soon as you leave the room?
V. Bright

Questionnaire
Part 2

Experiment B
Size of Opening: 100cmX100cm

Name of Interviewee:
Louis Ibrahim

Part B: Entering the Box

4. How do you feel as you enter the room?
hot and dark
5. What do you see?
a table
6. Are you comfortable?
i guess

Part C: Sitting at the Desk

6. Can you see me clearly?
Yes
7. Can you read the newspaper on the desk?
Yes
8. Do you want to switch an artificial light?
Yes
9. Do you want to open a window?
Yes
10. Do you want to have a view?
Yes

Part D: Exiting the Box

2. How do you feel as soon as you leave the room?
Still bright, better than before

Questionnaire
Part 2

Experiment C
Size of Opening: 200cmX200cm

Name of Interviewee:
Lamis Ibrahim.

Part B: Entering the Box

7. How do you feel as you enter the room?
Warm /

8. What do you see?
table

9. Are you comfortable?
Yes

Part C: Sitting at the Desk

11. Can you see me clearly?
Yes

12. Can you read the newspaper on the desk?
Yes

13. Do you want to switch an artificial light?
Yes

14. Do you want to open a window?
Yes

15. Do you want to have a view?
No - This is sufficient.

Part D: Exiting the Box

3. How do you feel as soon as you leave the room?
Not that different

Made in the USA
Monee, IL
15 February 2021

60526455R00128